THE
GRAND
PARENTS
HANDBOOK

For my father, Arthur Trostler, who would have been an amazing grandfather.

Copyright © 2009 by Elizabeth LaBan

All rights reserved. No part of this book may be reproduced in any form without written permission from the publisher.

Library of Congress Cataloging in Publication Number: 2009927563

ISBN: 978-1-59474-412-9

Printed in Singapore

Typeset in Monoline Script, Helvetica Neue, and Century Schoolbook

Designed by Jenny Kraemer
Illustrations by Sean Sims, represented by New Division
Production management by John J. McGurk

Distributed in North America by Chronicle Books
680 Second Street
San Francisco, CA 94107

10 9 8 7 6 5 4 3 2 1

Quirk Books
215 Church Street
Philadelphia, PA 19106
www.irreference.com
www.quirkbooks.com

THE
GRAND PARENTS
HANDBOOK

GAMES, ACTIVITIES, TIPS, HOW-TOS, *AND* ALL-AROUND FUN

By Elizabeth LaBan

WITH NANA BARBARA TROOTLER
AND GRANDPA MYRON LABAN

QUIRK BOOKS
PHILADELPHIA

Table of Contents

Introduction
The Magic of Grandparenthood   7

    On Becoming a Grandmother, by Nana Barbara 10
    On Becoming a Grandfather, by Grandpa Myron 12

I.   Bringing Up Baby
A Grandparent's Refresher Course   16

    How to Change a Diaper 18
    Six Ways to Soothe a Crying Baby 21
    Chicken Soup for the New Parents' Soul 23
    How to Swaddle a Baby 24
    Baby Burping 101 26
    Baby Food for Beginners 27
    Baby Medicine Basics 29
    How to Baby- and Kid-Proof Your Home 30
    Useful Equipment for Grandma's House 33
    Safe Sleeping Arrangements 35
    Nursery Rhyme Time 36
    Games Babies Play 40
    A Babysitting Primer 44
    Splish-Splash Bath-Time Fun 46
    Handling Toddler Tantrums 50
    How to Give a Modern-Day Time-Out 52
    When Siblings Fight 54

II. Indoor and Outdoor Fun and Games   58

Hold a Backyard Olympics 60
A Guide to Camping in the Great Indoors 66
Plan a Scavenger Hunt 69
Top 5 Ways to Survive a Car Trip. 71
Hold Your Own Horse Race 74
Four-Leaf Clover Hunting 78
Sardines in a Can and Clothespin Tag 79
Play Pirate for a Day. 81
Plant Fairy and Goblin Gardens 85
Hold a Spring-Cleaning Yard Sale 88
Hold a Mock Election. 90
Take a Trip to the Toy Store. .92

III. Crafts and Cooking   94

Sugar Fixes: Foolproof Cookie Recipes. 96
Sew a Family Crazy Quilt 99
The Scoop: Creating a Family Newspaper 103
Fruit Picking and the Secrets to Amazing Cobbler 105
Create Your Own Ice-Cream Cake 107
The Secrets to Delicious Homemade Pickles 109
Fun and Games with the Family Photo Album. 112
Collections and Crafting with Collections 114
Discover a New Language by Compiling a
    Picture Dictionary 119
Make a Holiday Dinner Centerpiece 121
Bring On the Bead People 123
Fuse Bead Fun 126
Easy-as-Pie Apple Crumb Pie 128
Top 10 Greatest Snacks of All Time 130

Make a Good-Times Diorama 138
Create a Family Fun Box 141
Build a Gingerbread House 143
Fun-with-Paper Projects 145
Afternoon Tea and Scone Treats 150

IV. *Sharing and Exploring the World Together*   154

Make Trail Mix and Hit the Trails! 156
Top 10 Tips for a Day at the Museum or Zoo 158
Dining Out, Kid-Style: A Survival Guide 161
A Visit from the Tooth Fairy 163
Top 4 Tricks to Staying in Touch with
    Your Grandchildren 165
Travel Through Time Together 168
Take a Ride on a Train or Bus 171
Yellow Light Activities: When to Proceed with Caution . . . 172
Visiting Your Grandchild's Classroom 174
Tips for School Pickup Days 176
Plan a Special Meal Together 178
Create Your Family Tree 180
Top 10 Books to Read to Your Grandchildren 183
Open Up a Bank Account for Your Grandchild 186
The Top 10 Questions Every Grandchild Asks 187

Metric Conversion Charts 191

Introduction
The Magic of Grandparenthood

I knew from the moment my mother first laid eyes on my inconsolable newborn daughter Alice that there was magic between them. The brand-new grandmother came to the hospital all dressed up, having carefully chosen the softest sweater in her closet. She took Alice into her arms and just stared at her for what must have been more than an hour. The funny thing is, Alice stared back. The whole time. For most of her first week of life, Alice cried and cried. But when my mother held her, this tiny newborn was more peaceful than at any other time. Frankly, I would have given anything to switch places with my mother. But that wasn't what my mother wanted this time around. She wanted to be the grandmother.

What I was observing was an incredible gift. In one moment, Alice had gained an experienced, gentle, and, most of all, patient caregiver, just when we needed her most. It's that gift, as well as those of each of my children's grandparents, that inspired me, my mother, and my father-in-law to write this book.

As we gathered many of the activities and advice for this book, my mother and father-in-law spoke with grandparents throughout the country, some of whom live close to their grandchildren, others who live far away. They discussed what they wished they had known before they assumed their roles as grandparents, what their favorite memories are, and what they wished they had done differently. More than any single thing, every grandparent said they wished they had spent more time with their grandchildren. They had learned that doing things together is so much more important than giving gifts. They had learned that the shared time with their grandchildren was the true gift.

This book offers you endless ideas about how to spend that special time with your grandchildren and to create memories you will all hold on to, whether you're taking care of the newborn's practical day-to-day needs or embarking on an outdoor adventure with a toddler who can walk and talk. You'll learn again how to bathe and swaddle a baby and what to avoid feeding a child younger than one year old. (Some of these practices may have changed since you raised your own kids.) You'll also discover new activities, like planting a goblin garden or making a family tree, and rediscover the joys of cooking up family recipes that have been passed down through the generations.

Nine years after her first meeting with Alice, my mother still can't get enough of her grandchildren. When I bring home my son Arthur's school folder, barely glancing at the pages inside because I have to make dinner or answer e-mails or steal a few minutes to write, my mother will slowly and carefully go through each page, reading and absorbing what he learned. If Alice has to practice the piano or her multiplication tables, my mother sees helping as an honor, never a chore. When I am rushed or angry or bored, my mother and my in-laws are not. There are no e-mails or dinners or stories to write that could possibly be more interesting than their grandchildren. (Truth be told, my father-in-law has been known to be distracted by a broken garage door opener or a weed problem in his garden now and then, but he would do anything for his five grandchildren.)

Being a grandparent is not always easy. You have to navigate the parents' relationships to get to know their children. You might find that you've offended your son or daughter when you thought you were just acting in your grandchild's best interest. Other times, you have to figure out what your grandchildren care about, what they think about, what they want to know more about and spend their time doing. And these interests can change dramatically from visit to visit, and from child to child.

As my father-in-law says, he planned extensively to be a father, but becoming a grandfather just happened. He didn't have a chance to prepare. Here's your chance. This book is full of tips and useful tools to help you on your way. I hope it brings joy and extra magic to the time you spend with your grandchildren. Welcome to grandparenthood!

On Becoming a Grandmother
By Nana Barbara (aka Barbara Trostler)

Second only to the incredible happiness I experienced at the birth of my daughter came the exciting births of my two grandchildren, Alice and Arthur. Another world opened up to me. These were my daughter's and her husband's babies, and I could love them and hug them and love them some more!

Certainly, there were also those moments when the memories about what it really takes to get a fussy newborn to sleep came rushing back. Anyone reading this book, I'm sure, will recall walking back and forth, back and forth, with that tiny baby, trying everything in your repertoire to get her to sleep. And then, all of a sudden, there's the moment when that tiny body becomes heavy, and you know sleep has come. It's a delightful feeling.

As my grandchildren grew older, bedtimes remained a very special time whenever I visited. I loved reading an alphabet book to Alice, and I would watch her eyes grow heavy and close and open and smile at me and close again. I would sing songs to my grandchildren that my own parents had sung to me. (I'm certainly not a singer, but my grandchildren have never seemed to care.)

Even when I have gone about the less-than-glamorous duties in my role as grandmother, there have always been times, especially when my grandchildren were still fairly small, when I knew they genuinely liked me. And not only that, they loved me! I would tell my friends how I kept saying that to myself, and think how absolutely wonderful this adventure is.

This book is intended to remind you to cherish your own precious times with your treasured grandchildren. In it you'll find the many common threads and themes we encountered when we spoke to grandparents everywhere. The activities and ideas for sharing experiences with this newest generation will, ideally, inspire you to recall the ones you shared with your own grandparents, parents, and children.

Alice, Arthur, my daughter, and I recently made an apple pie together, and the memories of my helping my grandmother bake pies came flooding back to me. I've been fortunate to come to know that there's no better way to span the generations than through the wonders of these passed-down traditions.

On Becoming a Grandfather
By Grandpa Myron (aka Myron LaBan)

*B*ecoming a father is usually a rational, participatory act. Becoming a grandfather is, at best, an irrational one: Without anyone asking your permission or advice, you suddenly find yourself cohabiting with a grandmother. But like fatherhood itself, dealing with a first grandchild is a new adventure. Traditionally, new grandparents have relied on on-the-job training to get into the swing of their new role, but with this book, we, as seasoned grandparents and parents, hope to ease your transition. In the chapters that follow, we provide commonsense advice and ideas drawn from our combined years of experience, as well as that of grandparents we interviewed far and wide.

First, some basic perspectives. It's important to remember that even as you indulge in the dynastic joys of nurturing a child that shares one-quarter of your genetic makeup, your new role can be fraught with unpredictable forms of political intrigue. Advice to the new mother, for example, even though well intended, may be less than appreciated by your daughter or daughter-in-law. Comparing your son or son-in-law's parenting skills to your own will invariably get you into hot water as well. Remember to tread with care when it comes to offering opinions. (Particularly in the early months with a newborn, even well-intended suggestions can sound like criticism.)

Each stage in your relationship with this new child will no doubt bring back many memories of what it was like to be a parent. Prepare yourself: Once you've survived the early years of dutifully watching, often for many hours, the wondrous play of your infant grandchild, you will now be regaled by the intimate details of his or her toilet training—often at the dinner table! Later, you'll learn to contend with the fact that your "genius" grandchild, initially so precociously dexterous with educational toys, is actually just like his peers in the nursery-school classroom when it comes to his extraordinary gifts. (And you will accept that this is just as it should be.)

Soon enough—just when the child is mastering the fine arts of communication—she'll transform once again: this time into an adolescent with a hectic schedule that allows little time for visiting with the old folks. In no time at all, having funded your own child's college education, graduate school, wedding reception, and perhaps even a first mortgage, you may find yourself—if you're fortunate enough to have the resources—gratefully taking on a new role as the primary contributor to your grandchild's college fund.

In all of these journeys, you will find a path well traveled by other grandparents. With this book in your hands, we hope their guidance will serve to enlighten and energize both those whose travels are still incomplete and those whose adventure is about to begin.

Grandparent Wisdom

WHAT ARE SOME OF THE DOS AND DON'TS YOU LEARNED AS A GRANDPARENT?

" Do give lots of hugs and kisses—start doing this when they're very young. Don't correct them in front of their parents. "

—Lois, grandmother of 6

" Don't try to parent them instead of grandparenting them. "
—Bonnie, grandmother of 3

" When greeting your family, kiss your daughter [or son] first, before your grandchildren. "

—Judy, grandmother of 4

" Engage yourself in activities your grandchildren enjoy: sports, arts, reading. Activities build a wonderful bond. "

—Bernie, grandfather of 1

" Don't overrule something that a parent has said. Never indulge a grandchild and then say, "But don't tell your parents. "

—Mary Ellen, grandmother of 3

" Don't interfere when parents are disciplining. Do give advice when asked for it. "

—Nancy, grandmother of 5

" Do: Love them, and hug them, without smothering them. Make memories with activities suitable for their ages. Spend as much time as you can with them. Teach them about your family history. Be honest with advice but don't criticize the parents. Give material things within reason. Teach good manners and thank-you note etiquette. Don't: Take sides; remain neutral, but give advice when asked. "

—Fran, grandmother of 3

" Do be yourself. Be generous in showing love and affection with hugs and kisses. Don't overdo it if it embarrasses children. Don't contradict parents' rules and discipline. Don't worry about competing with other grandparents; grandchildren have limitless love! "

—Nancy, grandmother of 4

" Do be supportive, and don't be judgmental. Long hair, loud music [are all phases] that will pass! "

—Harriet, grandmother of 4

" Do remember their birthdays. Do love them unconditionally Do laugh at their jokes. Do give lots of hugs. Don't try to take parents' role. "

—Marjorie, grandmother of 9

" Try to be democratic, especially when giving gifts; make sure they are all equivalent. "

—Robert, grandfather of 3

Bringing Up Baby
A Grandparent's Refresher Course

*F*irst-time grandparents often feel they don't have much to worry about regarding the basics of baby care. After all, you did all the diapering, feeding, sleep training, and child-proofing with your own kids, so how hard could it be? Your hard-won baby-care expertise will be invaluable to your children and grandchildren, but there will be those times when your daughter hands over her new daughter and asks you to change one of those newfangled earth-friendly diapers and you can't figure out which end is up. Or your son begs you to hold his crying newborn so that he and your daughter-in-law can rest for just a few minutes—an hour at the most—and the baby just won't stop crying. You might remember exactly what you did to soothe that long ago inconsolable infant (the one who just thrust his own baby at you), but it might also seem like eons ago and be hard to dredge up your strategies in a pinch.

Relax, take a deep breath, and read through the baby- and toddler-care refresher course that follows. Some of these techniques and tips might jog your memory in an instant; others might seem completely unfamiliar. But in no time you'll be an old pro again.

The best part? Even if your grandchild doesn't stop crying or refuses to go to sleep, you'll be able to return her to her parents and let them take over!

How to Change a Diaper

*Y*ou probably haven't changed a diaper in years—and if you're a grandfather of a certain generation, maybe you've never changed one at all. But that's no reason to be intimidated. Thanks to the miracle of disposable, folded diapers and baby wipes, changing a baby is easier than ever.

Of course your children may be trying to help the environment by doing things the old-fashioned way—with cloth diapers, safety pins, and endless trips to the washing machine. If that's the case, ask them to consider a temporary switch to disposable diapers while you babysit. If they protest, tell them you're out of practice and afraid of accidentally sticking the baby with a safety pin. That should do the trick.

What you will need:

★ Changing station
★ Clean diaper
★ Baby wipes
★ Diaper cream
★ Plastic bag for the dirty
  diaper

1 Assemble your supplies. If you're visiting the baby's house, simply locate the changing station and confirm that all of the items listed are present. If the baby is visiting your house, you may want to set up a temporary changing station during the visit. You can purchase a changing pad at a store, although a large towel placed on a bed works just as well. Whatever you do, remember: *Never* leave a baby unattended on a changing table.

2 Open the clean diaper and place it to the side.

3 Lay the baby on his back and remove his pants.

4 Open the used diaper—slowly.

5 If the diaper is wet, simply fold it over and put it out of reach. Use one wipe to clean the baby's bottom.

6 If the diaper is soiled, lift the baby's ankles to access and clean his bottom. This will likely require several wipes. If your grandchild is a girl, take extra care to wipe from front to back. Drop the used wipes on top of the open dirty diaper, covering some of the mess.

7 When the baby's bottom is clean enough to rest on the towel or pad, fold the dirty diaper (using the Velcro bands to seal it tight) and put it in the waiting plastic bag or at least off to the side.

8 Liberally apply diaper cream to irritated areas (unless your children have specifically instructed you otherwise).

9 Gently lift the baby's ankles and slide the clean diaper under his bottom.

10 Lower the baby's legs and fold up the front flap, then fasten the side tabs of

the diaper (these will be sticky or Velcro). You should be able to slip one finger between the diaper and the baby's tummy. Don't make it any looser or it may fall off.

11 Dress the baby and dispose of the diaper. If the diaper is soiled, you may wish to carry it to an outdoor trash can (once the baby is safely in a crib, of course).

12 Wash your hands thoroughly.

Be Careful!

Some babies will push their feet into the poop before you have a chance to stop them. If this happens, use wipes to thoroughly clean their feet. In addition, boys occasionally pee while their diapers are off. If you are concerned, add a cloth diaper to your supplies and place it over the baby's penis as you change him.

Six Ways to Soothe a Crying Baby

*D*o you remember the first days after you brought your newborn son or daughter home from the hospital? Well now that child's become a parent—one who may need your baby-caretaking skills from time to time so that she can take a well-deserved break from parental duties. This is where Grandma and Grandpa really get to shine.

Even if memories of your baby's early infanthood have faded, you'll likely remember this basic fact: All babies cry. They cry when they're cold, hot, hungry, dirty, wet, and sometimes out of sheer boredom or frustration. Here's a quick refresher course in some sure-fire soothing techniques. Try one, or try them all in succession. One way or another, you will eventually hit on the solution (and maybe even be rewarded with a grateful smile).

1 Change the baby's diaper. A wet or soiled diaper may be causing discomfort. Take your time cleaning the baby, talking to her all the while and applying some soothing diaper ointment. Babies love to be tended to.

2 Rock her in your arms or put her firmly over your shoulder, letting the baby's stomach rest there. She may enjoy the change of scenery.

3 If she's feeling gassy, a slight bit of pressure on her belly might relieve some of the discomfort. Lay the baby gently on her back (on a blanket on the floor or on the bed) and very gently move her little legs in a bicycle-riding motion. This might help relieve some of the bloating.

4 Walk the baby around in your arms, swaying back and forth, or rock her in a chair.

If it's a nice day, consider going outside for a walk.

5 Use soothing sounds such as songs, gentle humming, or even the white noise of a dishwasher or electric fan. For some babies, nothing works better than being strapped securely in a car seat for a "ride" atop a running washing machine or dryer.

6 Offer a pacifier to suck or the tip of your pinky finger (after washing your hands thoroughly). This might just provide enough comfort to take the edge off. (Note: Some parents choose to wait before introducing a pacifier, but if your grandchild is already using one, make sure you always have several of her favorites handy.)

Grandparents' Note

At times, no matter what soothing techniques you try, the baby will continue to cry. Simply do the best you can to comfort her. If you find yourself becoming increasingly frustrated, put the baby down in a safe place such as the crib for a few minutes while you collect yourself.

Chicken Soup for the
New Parents' Soul

*A*s a grandparent, you are uniquely equipped to nourish your son's or daughter's new family. While they're busy trying to figure out how to feed the baby, they won't be giving much thought to how they're going to feed themselves. But eat they must: Sleep deprivation, nursing, and caring for other children require that parents of newborns recharge and refuel to get through these early days.

If you live nearby or will be visiting when the new baby arrives, cook and freeze in advance as many meals as you can. Make simple things that everyone will eat and that are easy to reheat and serve: soups, pasta casseroles, plain pasta, meat loaf, washed and prepared salad greens.

If you live far away, do some simple meal preparation during your first visit. Then gather take-out menus from local restaurants so you can order food for the new parents once a week for as long as your budget allows. This will be a most welcome gift.

How to Swaddle a Baby

*O*nce your own child grew to adulthood, you probably had a few pangs of nostalgia over missing the lovely, sweet sensation of holding a tiny baby in your arms. As a grandparent, you get to experience that pleasure all over again while also providing a set of extra arms when your son or daughter needs them most.

Get back into practice with some basic swaddling techniques to help your grandchild feel cozy and secure. She just spent nine months growing inside a very small area, so swaddling is an ideal way to make her feel especially comfortable. As an added benefit, swaddling keeps the baby's arms at her sides so she won't scratch herself or startle herself awake.

1 Locate a baby or receiving blanket. The hospital-issue variety works well for this purpose.

2 Place the blanket on a flat, secure expanse, such as a bed or the floor.

3 Arrange the blanket so that one corner points upward; fold down that corner roughly 4 to 5 inches.

4 Place the baby on the blanket with her head just above the fold. The tops of her shoulders should be level with the top of the blanket.

5 Fold over the left side of the blanket as tightly as you can, making sure the baby's right arm is comfortable and close to her body.

6 Gently hold the baby's left arm above the blanket and tightly secure the blanket under the baby's back.

7 Fold up the bottom corner, securing it with the final flip of the blanket.

8 Fold the right side of the blanket, this time making sure the baby's left arm is comfortable and close to her body as the blanket is tucked under behind her back.

Baby Burping 101

*A*s you no doubt recall from endless nights with a colicky or gassy baby, there is no greater relief for fussiness than a good, loud, satisfying burp. Babies' digestive systems are immature, and they tend to have some discomfort from swallowing air while nursing or taking a bottle. Be sure to have a cloth diaper or soft hand towel handy when you sign on for baby-feeding duty. Toss the cloth over your shoulder to protect your clothes in case the baby spits up. Try any of these techniques to elicit a burp each time you give your infant grandchild a bottle:

* Position the baby over your shoulder or on a slight diagonal, with the baby's stomach against your chest and his head resting on your shoulder. Gently pat his back and rub in circular upward motions.
* Sit the baby on your lap, facing away from you, and pat his back with gentle but firm strokes. Be sure to support the head.
* Lay the baby across your lap, with his head resting on your leg, and pat his back with firm but gentle pressure.

Grandparents' Note

If the baby doesn't burp but still seems fussy, you can always try again in a few minutes. If no burp is produced, be sure to mention it to the parents. They may want to consult the doctor if it happens frequently. Extreme fussiness after eating may be a sign of lactose intolerance or another reaction to food.

Baby Food for Beginners

*O*nce a baby is started on solid foods, there are a few things to keep in mind when caring for the child in your home. Doctors have a short list of foods that babies should not be introduced to during their first year due to the possibility of allergic reaction or the young body's inability to process certain substances. These include

- ★ Peanuts and peanut butter
- ★ Citrus fruit and juice
- ★ Strawberries
- ★ Chocolate
- ★ Honey
- ★ Cow's milk
- ★ Nuts (especially if allergies run in the family)
- ★ Shellfish

Always be sure to cut foods into small pieces to avoid choking. For a baby under one year, a good rule of thumb is to keep everything pea-sized. Here are a few potentially hazardous foods that should be either avoided entirely or cut up especially well before serving.

- ✳ Grapes (and cherry tomatoes) must be cut into quarters, from babyhood well into toddlerhood.
- ✳ Popcorn should not be offered the first three or four years.
- ✳ Hard candies should be avoided; they can easily lodge in the child's throat.
- ✳ Large gummy candies and marshmallows should be cut up or avoided entirely.
- ✳ Sausage and hotdogs should be cut lengthwise before being cut into smaller pieces.

* All meat should be cut into very small pieces.
* Peanut butter (when the child is old enough to eat it) should be spread thinly on bread; add jelly to help soften the texture and make it easier to eat.
* Cheese sticks and other chewy snacks should be eaten with care.

Be Aware!

Make sure the child is always seated when she eats, and never give her food to eat in the car. Stopping short might startle her and cause her to choke.

Baby Medicine Basics

*B*abysitting your grandchild is one of life's most satisfying experiences, but sometimes that sweet bundle of joy will show signs she's not feeling so well. Without the words to tell you what's going on, she will need you to be the first line of defense until her parents return. Be prepared with all the information you'll need to take care of a sick child, whether in her home or yours.

1 Have the parents write down their cell-phone numbers as well as contact info for the child's doctor and the closest hospital emergency room (with directions to each).

2 Have the parents orient you to the location of the thermometer, humidifier, and any basic medications you need to use while they're away.

3 Have them write down the baby's/child's weight so that you can accurately give fever-reducing medicine only if you are directed to do so.

Be alert to the warning signs of serious illness or injury. Get the child to the emergency room right away when:

* The child's fever is over 105°F rectally
* The child has a seizure
* The child seems to be in severe pain or is clearly dehydrated
* The child has trouble breathing
* The child's skin looks purplish and mottled
* The child's neck is clearly stiff
* Your gut instinct tells you something is wrong

How to Baby- and Kid-Proof Your Home

*I*t's probably been a long while since you had to worry about child-proofing your home, but crawling babies and small children can get into trouble fast. The safer your house is for visits, the more comfortable you and your children will be about your hosting your grandchild on your own turf.

The good news is that baby- or child-proofing your house is quite instinctual. Simply get down on your hands and knees and crawl around slowly to view your home from a little tot's point of view. (Remember: From the time babies can crawl until they are about two years old they will put *everything* in their mouths.) The hazards will be immediately apparent, and then you can set about securing them. Much of this work can be done without investing a lot of money or permanently changing your living space.

> ## Be aware!
> ....
> Nothing keeps a baby or young child safer than adult supervision, so even if you think your house is safe, keep your eyes and ears on the little one at all times.

1 Put away all items that are small, breakable, or choking hazards. Pebbles, jewelry, buttons, pills, coins, and the like should be stored out of child's reach.

2 Plug unused electric sockets with plastic safety-

outlet inserts (available at most hardware stores).

3 Secure the stairs that will be in your grandchild's play and sleep areas by installing temporary safety gates that can be stashed away when not in use. In a pinch, you can block unsecured stairways with a heavy piece of furniture, *but you will need to watch the baby at all times.* Children on the go are enormously resourceful climbers, so don't risk a serious fall by letting them out of your sight, even for a moment.

4 Block and lock your laundry chute.

5 Make sure that heavy furniture is anchored to the wall and that televisions and other appliances are secure so that they cannot be pulled down by little hands.

6 Install guards and/or stops to reduce the risk of the child falling from your

windows. Be sure that you can easily unlock the stops in case of an emergency.

7 Make sure to keep all cribs and children's beds away from windows and blinds. Curious children love to play with the pulls and cords, so take care to secure them out of reach or inside a plastic safety holder, to avoid strangulation.

8 Remove fireplace tools and store them in a secure closet. Install a fireplace barrier so the child cannot access the area. Pad the hearth with blankets or invest in a padded hearth guard to cushion the area in case of a fall.

9 Lock the cleaning-supply, medicine, and liquor cabinets or move the items to a higher location out of the child's reach.

10 Keep toilet seats down and bathrooms secured when not in use, to

avoid accidental drowning. It may sound unlikely, but small children—particularly crawling babies who can pull themselves to stand—are especially at risk for this hazard.

11 Keep knives and matches out of reach at all times.

12 Use locks that are out of the child's reach or install a chain high on your entryway doors so that a child can't leave your home without your knowledge.

Useful Equipment
for Grandma's House

*W*hen you're expecting your children and grandchildren for a long weekend visit, you can ease their burden by procuring a few basic items they'd otherwise have to carry with them. This equipment is a great investment since you'll be able to use it every time you take care of the little ones for either a night or an extended stay

Car seat. If you're picking up the family at the airport, it will be enormously helpful to come with a car seat already installed. Borrow one from friends, rent one from a car-rental place, or simply purchase one if you'll get more than a couple uses out of it. Make sure the seat is age-appropriate for your grandchildren and properly installed (rear-facing until at least age one). If your children are driving to your home, make sure to transfer their car seats to your car before they take off.

Portable bed or crib. Don't set up a dusty old crib that's been stashed in your basement since your youngest child moved to a big bed. Most likely it will not meet current safety standards. You can buy a collapsible, portable crib at most baby stores for very little money; it can also serve as a safe place to set the baby when you need to go to the bathroom or answer the door or phone. For older grandchildren, push a bed against a wall and install safety railings.

Bouncy seat. This small, slinglike seat is another good place to put the baby while you make dinner, and it will also help occupy and soothe him. Many seats come with settings for seat vibrations or music playing; some also have toy bars the child can bat at. You might also consider buying a floor mat or baby gym or, as he gets a little older, an "exersaucer" that allows the baby to stand safely and play with the toys around him.

Assorted baby supplies. Blankets, pacifiers, diapers and diaper pail, wipes, baby soap and shampoo, baby spoons and cups, booster seat, and bibs are all useful to have on hand. Check with the parents for preferred brands.

Safe Sleeping Arrangements

*Y*ou probably have fond memories of gently placing your infant on his stomach and tucking him in with a soft blanket for the night. Times have changed: Beginning in 1994, pediatricians began to advocate the "Back to Sleep" program to reduce the incidence of Sudden Infant Death Syndrome (SIDS). It's now considered safest to place babies on their backs, without blankets or pillows that might block airways, when putting them down to sleep. Here's how to make your grandchild's sleeping arrangements as safe as possible.

1 Make sure the baby's crib is up to current safety standards: The mattress should be new, clean, and firm, and the crib should conform to the latest guidelines for slat positioning. (The slats of many older cribs are positioned too far apart, making it possible for the baby's head to get caught between.) You can buy inexpensive collapsible, portable cribs for the occasional baby guest.

2 The sleeping area should be kept clear of anything—pillows, quilts, toys— that could block the baby's face or hinder movement. (Infants are unable to turn their heads away from a suffocation hazard.)

3 Make sure the baby is not overdressed and that the room is not overheated. A light cotton sleeper in summer and a heavier fleecy one in winter should be sufficient.

4 If you are not within earshot of the room where the baby is sleeping, invest in a basic baby monitor. Basic, inexpensive units allow you to hear what's going on while carrying on around the house.

Nursery Rhyme Time

*C*hildren love to hear stories about what their parents were like as children, and small children in particular love repetition (*"Again,* Grandpa!"). What better way to offer both treats than by regaling them with the nursery rhymes and games you sang and played with their parents? The rhymes below are sure to bring back memories—and hopefully help make some new ones. If you want to add some fun, act out the rhymes with pantomimes, funny voices, exaggerated expressions, and finger movements. Some suggestions are provided in the "stage directions" that follow.

Little Miss Muffet

> *Little Miss Muffet*
> *Sat on a tuffet,*
> *Eating her curds and whey,*
> *Along came a spider,*
> *Who sat down beside her,*
> *And frightened Miss*
> *   Muffet away.*

Stage directions:

1 Stand across from your grandchild or, if there is a group of children, have them stand in a circle. When Miss Muffet sits, you sit down; when she eats, you pretend to eat.

2 When the spider comes along, spread out and wiggle your fingers like a spider, or pretend your hand is a spider crawling across the floor.

3 When Miss Muffet is frightened away, run from the circle in mock fright.

Humpty Dumpty

*Humpty Dumpty sat on
a wall,
Humpty Dumpty had
a great fall,
All the king's horses and
all the king's men,
Couldn't put Humpty
together again.*

Stage direction:
You know what to do! Fall down at the announcement of Humpty's great fall, then try (but fail) to stand up with the final verse.

Little Boy Blue

*Little Boy Blue,
Come, blow your horn.
The sheep's in the meadow,
The cow's in the corn.
Where is the little boy
Who looks after the sheep?
Under the haystack
Fast asleep.*

Stage directions:
Given the sleepy theme of this rhyme, it's perfect for creating a bedtime ritual when your grandchildren sleep over.

1 Mime blowing a horn in the first line.

2 Act out the sheep and the cow, searching through the meadow for the boy.

3 Drop your head forward to pretend to be falling "fast asleep."

Rings on Her Fingers

Ride a cock horse
To Banbury Cross,
To see a fair lady,
Ride a white horse.
Rings on her fingers,
And bells on her toes,
And she shall have music
Wherever she goes.

Stage directions:
This is a great rhyme to recount while bouncing baby on your knees. Alternatively:

1 Pretend to hold the reins while riding a horse.

2 Wave your hands to show off the rings on your fingers and shake your feet to ring the bells on your toes.

3 Make-believe waltz to the tune.

Hey Diddle Diddle

Hey diddle diddle
The cat and the fiddle
The cow jumped over the
*   moon.*
The little dog laughed
To see such sport
And the dish ran away
*   with the spoon.*

Stage directions:
For small babies, you can mime the simple movements of playing a fiddle, jumping over the moon, and running away. If you have a group of older grandchildren:

1 Have them sit in a circle on the floor.

2 Assign a word to each child: cat, fiddle, cow, moon, dog, dish, spoon.

3 As you recite the rhyme together, each child stands, spins around, and then sits down again when you reach his or her assigned word.

The Noble Duke of York

Oh, the noble Duke of York
He had ten thousand men
He marched them up to the top of the hill
And he marched them down again.
Oh, when you're up, you're up
But when you're down, you're down
But when you're only halfway up, you're neither up nor down!

Stage direction:
This is a great rhyme to sing as you raise baby up and down on your lap along with the words.

Games Babies Play

*E*ntertaining a baby is one of the most satisfying of life's experiences. They are still so new to the world that every interaction with the loved ones around them is an opportunity to absorb and see new things, hear new sounds, and smell new scents. Here are a few classic baby games to give you a quick refresher on ways to entertain your new grandchild. Just keep in mind that simply walking around and talking to her, showing her things in your house or on the street, and holding her on your lap are all important ways to connect and have fun.

Peek-a-Boo

Six months and up

The traditional "hands in front of your face" version is tried and true, of course, but try engaging your grandchild with a few variations:

* Cover the baby's eyes with your hand or a napkin, then pull it away on "peek-a-boo!" (Depending on temperament and age, the baby may not like this variation as well as the original.)
* Hide a puppet behind your back or behind the baby's back and pull it out on "peek-a-boo." Then hide the puppet again, varying the places from which you reveal the puppet to keep the baby interested.
* Do the same with the baby's favorite stuffed animal and blanket.

Baby Drums

Once the baby can sit up—around seven months
Gather baby-safe spoons in a variety of materials: metal, plastic, and wood. Give the baby one spoon and encourage her to bang it on varied surfaces to see what different sounds she can make. Then have her try it with the other spoons to make different types of sounds. Finally, set the baby in a highchair or on the floor and let her "drum" the spoons on some plastic bowls or cups. (Just make sure she doesn't poke herself in the eye.)

Can You Pour?

Nine months and up
Babies love to pour, but they need practice to learn the skill. Give them a chance to learn by getting a little messy. You'll need some small plastic pitchers or plastic measuring cups and bowls, and something to pour (dry cereal, water, etc.).

* If you're playing in the kitchen, cover the kitchen table with newspaper to minimize cleanup. Spread out a few pitchers or cups with a little dried cereal in each and encourage the baby to pour from one cup to the other. Choose a cereal she might also like to eat so she can snack and play at the same time.
* If you're playing with water, put the baby in a swimsuit and sit her in an empty bathtub. Make sure the baby is stable sitting up, and stay with her at all times so that she doesn't hit her head on the hard surfaces. Offer her the cups and let her pour water from one cup to the other.

Head and Shoulders

Any age
If the baby is tiny or can't sit yet, play this game with him lying down. If he can sit, then sit facing him while you recite the words. Once your grandchild can stand, it's even more fun!

You sing the words:
Head, shoulders, knees and toes, knees and toes,
Head, shoulders, knees and toes, knees and toes,
And eyes and ears and mouth and nose,
Head shoulders, knees and toes, knees and toes.

Gently touch the correct part of the baby's body as you name it. If the baby is tiny, speak softly. If he is older, you can be more raucous. When he's old enough to stand on his own, encourage him to touch his own shoulders and knees as you make the calls.

Farm Game

Nine months and up
You'll need as many plastic and stuffed farm animals as you can find. Spread out the animals on the floor near the baby. Sing the words to "Old MacDonald":

Old MacDonald had a farm
Ee ay ee ay o
And on that farm he had a [fill in the animal]
Ee ay ee ay o

When you say the name of an animal, pick it up and dance it around, then hand it to the baby. Repeat with each animal in turn. As the baby gets older and more familiar with the game and the animals, let her try to pick the animal out of the group after you say the name.

How Big Is Baby?

Any age

Play this game with the baby lying on her back, sitting up, or standing, depending on her age. Ask excitedly, "How big is the baby?" Then either grasp her fingers and lift her arms over her head or lift your arms over your head and say, "Soooo big!" Repeat as desired. When your grandchild is older, encourage her to lift her own arms overhead when you say, "Soooo big!"

A Babysitting Primer

*B*eing completely responsible for your grandchild while the parents are out might seem daunting at first, especially if you live far away and don't get to babysit as often as you'd like or if this will be one of your first times alone with your grandchildren. Here are a few tips to help you through.

1 Locate all the important equipment before the parents leave. This might include anything from a pacifier to a special blanket to a baby monitor to a beloved stuffed animal, depending on your grandchild's age.

2 Have all important phone numbers handy: parents' cell phone; restaurant, house, or other venue where they'll be; pediatrician's; poison control; and the closest neighbor. Be sure you also know the local numbers for the police and fire departments.

3 Be prepared for an emergency. Think about how you would get the children out of the house quickly if you had to. Know where the fire extinguishers are. Know where their allergy medicines are kept. And know where a flashlight or candles and matches are in case of a loss of electricity.

4 For older children, have the parents set the bedtime before they leave and be sure they communicate it clearly to the children in your presence. That way, you won't have to feel like the bad guy. If (or, more likely, *when*) your grandchildren try to convince you to let them stay up later, you can either say you want to do what Mom and Dad said or let them stay up 10 or 15 minutes beyond the designated time.

5 Let the parents decide in your presence whether the children can watch television or play video games and for how long. Again, you can follow their rules to the letter or throw in just a few extra minutes of screen time for good measure.

6 Do something fun. Depending on your grandchildren's moods and ages, have a dance party or play board games. Games like Apples to Apples, Life, Clue, Monopoly, Sorry, and Othello are all good choices, and some have junior versions for younger children. Or play

Go Fish or Old Maid, or let the children teach you their favorite card game. You can start an ante of pennies. They will love it.

7 Do something special before bedtime that you suspect the parents don't usually do. Make the children hot milk or give them a tiny sweet (not chocolate and not too much—you don't want to get them too hyped up). Tell them a special story—maybe even one about when their parents were little. This is a chance to start your own bedtime tradition.

Splish-Splash Bath-Time Fun

*P*arents are often too busy with the simple tasks of daily life to bother to make the kids' bath time anything but an ordinary, get-the-job-done experience. But Grandma and Grandpa, you can do better. In fact, bathing is a terrific rainy-day activity when you have nothing else planned.

It's common for some kids to resist bathing, so here's where you get to be creative. Build a theme around the characters and stories your grandchildren love: fairies, superheroes, army men, ocean wildlife. Purchase a few safety-rated plastic toys that fit with the theme, and keep them on hand for the kids' next visit. Add some food coloring to your shopping list, and you will be ready to create some aquatic adventures.

Blue Beach-Bath Boogie

What you will need:

★ Blue food coloring
★ Portable CD player
★ Plastic beach toys
★ Plastic flowers

1 While your grandchild isn't looking, put a few drops of blue food coloring into the bath water as the tub is filling up. Begin with three to four drops, and add one drop at a time to deepen the color slowly.

2 Put your favorite tropical or Hawaiian-style music on the CD player. (Just make sure the player is safely away from the water—or simply set it outside the bathroom.)

3 Set the plastic flowers around the tub.

4 Dump in a few plastic beach toys—the kids *will* go crazy!

The Greatest Bath on Earth

What you will need:

★ Red and blue food coloring

★ Several colorful plastic rings from a stacking cone toy

★ Plastic toy circus animals (elephants, horses, lions, tigers, etc.)

★ Plastic microphone or hairbrush

1 Mix the red and blue food coloring to make purple tub water.

2 Using your best circus-barker voice, announce into the plastic mic that it's time for "The Greatest Show on Earth!"

3 Have your grandchildren make the elephants and other animals jump through the plastic rings as you scrub.

Watercolor Bath

1 Let your grandchildren add colors of their choosing to the tub water.

2 Place daubs of shaving cream in each plastic bowl, then add a bit of food coloring in different colors to each bowl.

3 Let the grandkids go to town painting the walls of the tub and tile.

4 Let them wash it all down with soapy washcloths.

A Floating Army

1 Mix the yellow, green, and red food coloring into the bath water to create a murky brown bath.

2 Surprise your grandchild by dumping in the plastic soldiers.

3 Once he's settled in with the toy soldiers, present him with the plastic tank toy. He'll never want to leave the tub!

The Restaurant Bath

1 As you run the bath, tell your grandchildren you're opening your own waterfront restaurant.

2 Dump in the plastic toy food and give them each a place setting of plastic cups and plates.

3 Let them serve each other food on the plates and fill their cups with bath water. Just make sure they don't actually drink it!

Grandparents' Note

It's generally best to leave the bathing to Mom and Dad tho first few weeks of a newborn's life, since your grandchild is not yet sitting up and his head control is lacking. But by all means use your best sponge-bath technique if baby gets himself into a messy situation (vomiting, explosive diaper, and the like). Make sure to use only baby soap (or a very gentle variety— no perfumes or deodorants) and warm (not hot) water. Once your grandchild can sit up (between six and nine months), invest in a bath seat or ring for your tub so that the baby can sit securely while you focus on washing and playing. Keep a firm hand on baby at all times so that he doesn't slip under the water or injure himself.

Handling Toddler Tantrums

*W*hen you're babysitting for a full day or longer, it's possible that your darling toddler grandchild will let loose with the loudest, most uncontrollable tantrum you've ever experienced. The good news is that you are not the main disciplinarian in the child's life. You want to be consistent, and you want what you say to mean something, but you can be a little softer than you might have been when your own son threw himself on the sidewalk and refused to move.

If you're in public, remove yourselves from the situation. Even if it means leaving a filled shopping cart or missing the end of story time, a change of venue is sometimes all a screaming child needs.

If you're with a group of children and leaving will ruin it for everyone, minimize the situation that led to the tantrum. If you said no to that second chocolate bar because you thought that's what the parents would want, you might want to reconsider, for everyone's sake. It's okay to give in every now and then, even though you may have never considered doing so as a parent.

If you feel you need to uphold a higher level of authority, and your grandchild isn't too far gone, offer a choice. Perhaps she became upset because you said she couldn't have a second treat; ask her if she would rather have the second treat now or later, for dessert. Whatever she chooses, stick to the decision and give her the treat as promised.

In every case, remain calm. Don't become frazzled if people are watching. Remind yourself that most of them have children and grandchildren of their own and have been in this exact situation themselves. Don't show anger toward your grandchild, even if you feel it; this will only make the situation worse, and you might feel embarrassed and guilty later. Be firm and feel free to explain to others that your grandchild is having a rough afternoon, but don't act like it's the end of the world.

If you're at home and a tantrum ensues, consider the cause. Is the child acting out because she doesn't want to share a toy, or was her older brother mean and her feelings were hurt? If the latter, she might need comfort from you to calm down. If the former, she might just need to be left alone to gain control of herself. Go about your business, but don't wander far. You don't want her to feel abandoned, but you do want her to feel in control of her immediate environment.

Tantrum Prevention 101

Preventing a tantrum may be harder for you than for a parent because you won't always know or be able to anticipate the cause. Here are simple prevention strategies:

* Try offering a cracker or quick snack at the first signs of a meltdown. Sometimes the cause is as simple as hunger. You'd be amazed how a little something in the belly can give a child a whole new attitude.
* If your grandchild is clearly beginning to get bored or antsy, switch to another activity or change your planned outing for the day.
* Try to distract your grandchild with a toy or book. Sometimes just offering to read a story is enough to calm a child. Or consider putting on a calming CD or DVD while you all take a breather.
* Tell stories of the child's own parent's tantrums, and feel free to embellish. He'll be laughing in no time!

How to Give a Modern-Day Time-Out

*W*hen your grandkids' parents are on the scene, always let them take the lead in imposing discipline, even if it may be difficult to simply stand by and observe. No doubt they'll employ some form of "time-out" (today's disciplinary tool of choice), which might not be the way you typically handled your kids when they acted up. The time-out physically removes the child from the immediate situation or conflict, with a waiting period before reentering the activity.

Do your best to reconcile your disciplinary style with that of the parents when your grandchildren are exclusively in your care. You can always adapt the time-out so that you can comply with the technique without making the punishment too harsh. All you're hoping for is to distract the child from whatever is causing the bad behavior and to let her know you noticed it.

Ask the parents what they usually do for time-out, and let them know you'll adapt it slightly (sort of a "time-out lite," for grandparents only!).

Whereas the parents will have a dedicated time-out location in their home—usually the bottom step of a staircase or a special chair—your goal will be simply to remove the child from the situation for a brief time. The time-out length is typically dictated by the child's age. A two-year-old would have a two-minute time-out, a three-year old a three-minute time-out, and so on.

You might remove her from the TV show she's watching or the game she's playing to walk outside with you for a few minutes, or you might sit together on the back porch for the allotted time. Perhaps you can have her help clean up in the kitchen after dinner or help you get the towels out of the dryer. Be as creative as you like. If you do choose to put your grandchild in a sitting time-out on her own, simply make sure that she is always in a safe place. Once the time-out period is over, welcome her back enthusiastically to the original activity.

When Siblings Fight

*I*f you had more than one small child growing up in your household, you probably remember that they frequently fought, and you most likely had some strategies for dealing with their battles. Even so, it might surprise you to see your precious, sweet grandchildren going at each other. Fighting is one of the things siblings are pretty much guaranteed to do. Although they may usually be on their best behavior in your presence, any time you spend more concentrated stretches with them (on vacation or a long visit), they are going to let down their guards and revert to their everyday habits. Use these suggestions to review some basic discipline strategies.

1 *Recognize that children fight when they get bored.* This is a good incentive to keep organized activities moving along, especially if your grandchildren are visiting for a few days and they start to miss their parents. That's not to say you can't spend some time sitting around the house reading or watching a movie together, but if you notice the kids getting agitated with each other, have something at the ready to jump into (a game, a walk, a visit to the library or bookstore).

2 *If a fight breaks out, give the kids a brief chance to work it out themselves.* They just might. But if it escalates or goes on for a few minutes, be prepared to step in.

3 *If one of the kids is clearly winning the battle, pull the other one gently into the next room.* She will probably go willingly to save face—and the other child won't protest because she'll think she won. Speak to each child separately to get their stories (you don't

need them disputing each other's version of events). Take your time. By the time you're finished talking to each child, both might have calmed down.

4 *If this doesn't work, insist that they spend time in separate rooms.* A little quiet time alone should dissipate the anger. Send one child to your bedroom and the other to the living room where they can read, draw, even watch television, as long as each child has the same activities available.

5 *After some time has passed, bring them back together, but don't make them talk about the fight.* Ideally, they'll be happy to see each other again. Don't remind them of the argument.

6 *If the fighting gets out of hand and nothing you do helps, keep them separated for longer or, as a final resort, call the parents to ask for advice.* If your grandchildren are really going at it in front of you, you can be certain they do so at home, too. Their parents will have a few ideas at the ready.

Grandparent Wisdom

WHAT'S THE ONE PIECE OF ADVICE YOU WISH YOU HAD KNOWN BEFORE YOU HAD GRANDCHILDREN?

❝ To just love them, and to babysit whenever possible. ❞

—Joanne, grandmother of 1

❝ To check with the parent before I give any correction about manners or table manners. ❞

—Lois, grandmother of 6

❝ To prepare yourself mentally and emotionally for the overwhelming love and affection you give them—as if they were your own. ❞

—Victor, grandfather of 3

❝ [That] spending time with them is more important than anything you can give them. ❞

—Bonnie, grandmother of 3

❝ To childproof your home and relax! ❞

—Margo, grandmother of 3

❝ To let them explore new activities and make simple mistakes in the learning process rather than being perfect and always a winner. ❞

—Bernie, grandfather of 1

" That they would be like a magnet and that I'd want to be with them all the time. "

—*Nancy, grandmother of 5*

" That memories are more important than things. Memories of activities you do together will last forever. Most gifts don't last or are quickly forgotten. "

—*Nancy, grandmother of 4*

" To remember that you are not the parents. Do not undermine their authority. "

—*Harriet, grandmother of 4*

" To give encouragement and support to the parents. "

—*Robert, grandfather of 3*

" To be ready to supply all the love and support for this child. Be so proud: It is the greatest joy on earth. "

—*Diana, grandmother of 4*

" To love them always, but not to be afraid to discipline them when they're in your care. To bake lots of cookies. "

—*Joyce, grandmother of 5*

" To keep your children's toys available so the grandchildren can see and enjoy what their parents played with. "

—*Joanne, grandmother of 1*

" To remember: You raised your kids; let them raise theirs! "

—*Judy, grandmother of 12*

Indoor and Outdoor Fun and Games

*A*s you move from parenthood to grandparenthood, your job description changes. Sure, you'll have to make sure the children are safe and warm and fed, but now your main goal is to *have fun* with these little people!

Whether you live in a small apartment with limited outdoor space or a huge home with a lawn, there is so much to do with your grandchildren, both indoors and out. In the pages that follow, you'll find suggestions for activities that can be tailored to whatever space is available. A backyard Olympics relay can easily be held at a nearby park, and you can design a large or small scavenger hunt for indoors or outdoors. You can plant a fairy or goblin garden on a corner of your yard or simply buy a few planting pots. And the grandkids will be pleasantly surprised to find that four leaf clovers can be spotted on any type of green space, whether it's a public picnic area or your private yard.

If you're looking for ways to make a car ride more fun, activities for a rainy day, or instructions for transforming yourselves into pirates for an afternoon, let the ideas in this chapter be just the beginning of the wonderful times you share with your grandchildren as you get down to the nitty-gritty of having fun together.

Hold a Backyard Olympics

*W*hether it's an off year for the winter or summer games or a year when the Olympics are going full-throttle on every screen, you can engage the grandkids in a bit of fun and exercise by holding your own outdoor competitions. There's no better way to get some fresh air, and what child could resist the prospect of winning a shiny gold medal? Once the games are complete, hold a medal ceremony and serve special foods from the host country. Making the medals and your own Olympic torch is half the fun of preparing for the games. Any game can be part of your backyard Olympics, as long as it has clear gold, silver, and bronze medal winners. Below are some suggestions to start you off.

The Medals

What you will need:

- ★ Gold, silver, and bronze metallic paper cupcake liners (one for each medal)
- ★ Two sheets each of red, white, and blue construction paper
- ★ Glue
- ★ Several dark markers
- ★ Roll of red or blue ribbon
- ★ Stapler

1 Flatten the cupcake liners with the colored side facing up to form the medals' bases.

2 Cut circles from the construction paper to fit into the center circle of the liners. You'll want the metallic border to show, so cut the circles small enough to retain a color frame.

3 Use the markers to draw pictures, designs, numbers (#1, #2, #3), or words (*Gold, Silver, Bronze*) on the construction paper circles.

4 Glue the circles to the centers of the liners.

5 Staple each end of a piece of cut ribbon to the top of the medal with sufficient length to garland around the winner's neck.

The Torch

What you will need:

* ★ One large piece of black construction paper
* ★ Two sheets each of yellow, orange, and red tissue paper
* ★ Tape or glue

1 Roll the black construction paper into a cone and secure it with tape or glue.

2 Stuff the cone with yellow, orange, and red tissue paper to create the flame.

3 Let the children take turns holding the torch as they march out to the yard or park. Don't be surprised if you attract the attention of other kids hoping to join the games!

Construction Paper Relay

1 Divide the children into two equal teams, designated by color (e.g., the Red Team and the Blue Team).

2 Use lengths of rope or sticks to mark the start and finish lines. (The distance between them should be set according to space available and the kids' capabilities.)

3 Give each starting player two 8½-by-11-inch pieces of the same color paper. (Red Team will have two pieces of red paper; Blue Team two pieces of blue.)

4 Have each player line up at the starting line, with their teammates falling in place behind them. When you say, "Go," each player will place one piece of paper in front of her, step on it, then place the second piece in front of her while leaning backward to retrieve the first piece. The players repeat the process all the way to the finish line, where they will then turn around and work their way back to the starting line.

5 Once back at the starting line, the first player taps the next person on the team, who then repeats the process of moving from start to finish and back again.

6 The first team to have all players make it back to the start is the winner. The runner-up gets the silver.

Note

You can also play this relay with just two contestants, with the first player to make it back to the start designated the winner.

Off or On?

1 Set out a large old beach towel or picnic blanket and have all the players stand on it.

2 You will serve as the "caller," but the players must do the *opposite* of what you say: When you yell, "Everybody off," the players are supposed to stay put; when you call "Everybody on," they must step off the blanket. Each player must listen carefully to your commands to know what *not* to do to stay in the game.

3 Eliminate players as they make the wrong move. The final player in the game gets the gold.

Popcorn Race

1 Use lengths of rope or sticks to mark the start and finish lines.

2 Give each player a paper plate with six kernels of popped corn.

3 Players should line up at the starting line, holding their plates in front of them. The goal is to be the first to run to the finish line and back without allowing a single kernel to blow off the plate.

The Great Fruit Roll

1 Bring a round piece of fruit and a pencil for each player. Choose a fruit that will roll well, but that isn't too fragile. Apples or oranges work best, but pomegranates or lemons would also do—and will make rolling them a bit more of a fun challenge.

2 Use lengths of rope or sticks to mark the start and finish lines. (The distance between them, again, should be set according to the space available and the kids' capabilities.)

3 Each player should stand at the starting line, with his fruit positioned directly on the line.

4 When you say, "Go," the players will use their pencils to roll their fruit to the finish line and back. The winner is the child who returns to the start line first.

Important Note

Players are allowed to use only the pencil to roll the fruit. Using hands or feet will result in immediate disqualification! If you wish, this game can also be set up as a relay if there's not enough room for each child to play at the same time.

Grandpa's Clothes

1 Grab a bagful of old clothes and accessories from your closet: slippers, hats, scarves, and neckties you no longer wear will work well.

2 Divide the clothes among the players so that each has the same number of items.

3 Use the spare scarves or ties to mark off the start and finish lines.

4 When you call, "Go," each player must put on all the items and run to the finish line and back, without anything falling off. If a player loses something along the way, then he must go back to the beginning and start again.

5 The first player to make it to the finish line and back is the winner.

Note

You can also play this game as a team relay: Each player returning to the finish line gives his clothes to the next team member, who must put them on and race to the finish line and back. The first team to have all their players return with their clothes intact wins.

A Guide to Camping in the Great Indoors

*I*t's true that fresh air, singing birds, and babbling brooks add something to the experience of camping, but if heading into the woods proves too tough an endeavor, don't let that stop you from camping with your grandchildren—*indoors*. All you really need are sleeping bags, flashlights, and ingredients for those delectable campfire treats: s'mores. Whether you do it on a rainy afternoon or during an actual sleepover, it will be a bonding experience your grandchildren will long remember.

If you have tents that can be easily erected inside your living room or family room, set them up. If not, simply move the furniture out of the way and distribute sleeping bags and flashlights to everyone. (Alternatively, you can build your own tents or forts using furniture and some blankets or sheets: Simply stretch the fabric from one chair or couch to the next, forming a perfectly pitched indoor tent.) Turn out the lights and let the kids have fun snaking in and out of the sleeping bags with their lights. Arrange the sleeping bags in a circle, with a pretend campfire in the middle, and regale them with a ghost story.

Ghostly Tales

Be sure to set the tone for your ghost story according to what's appropriate to your grandchildren's ages. It can be as thrilling or as silly as your group wants. Just make sure not to scare the youngest in the bunch.

1 Begin with a few sentences to set the scene and describe the characters in the story: *Jenny, Max, and Lu were camping one night in the dark woods when something approached their tent. The noise they heard reminded them of the time raccoons tried to break into their garbage cans at home. They huddled together. Suddenly everything was quiet. Max was about to make his way out of the tent to see if anything was there, and at that moment . . .*

2 Let the child to your right pick up the story where you left off.

3 When she's finished adding to the story, have the child to her right continue the tale.

4 Continue until everyone has had a chance to add to the story. Finish with a "The End!"

S'mores the Easy Way

What you will need:

★ 1 box of graham crackers
★ 4–5 bars of milk chocolate
★ 1 bag marshmallows

★ 1 cookie sheet
Makes 20–24 s'mores

1 Preheat oven to the broiler setting. Be very careful to keep the children away from the hot oven.

2 Break the graham crackers into squares and place them in even rows on the cookie sheet.

3 If you like your chocolate melted, place a small piece of chocolate on top of each cracker, followed by one marshmallow. If you want to be more authentic, just place one marshmallow on top of each cracker.

4 Place the cookie sheet on a rack near the broiler, but be sure that the marshmallows do not touch the heating element. It takes only a few seconds for marshmallows to brown; they burn quickly.

5 Remove the sheet from the oven.

6 If you have already added the chocolate, simply cover each s'more with another cracker square. If not, place a piece of chocolate over the hot marshmallow and cover it with a cracker square.

7 Allow the s'mores to cool and then transfer them to a plate. If you can stand the possibility of a mess, let the children eat them on the floor in their sleeping bags.

Plan a Scavenger Hunt

*Y*our grandchildren probably appreciate a challenge, and kids always love hunting for hidden treasure. If you have a free afternoon or an hour before dinner, plan a scavenger hunt to pass the time. The hunt can take place indoors or out, depending on the weather and the children's ages. You might want to prepare an inside list and an outside list to plan for any contingency. If the hunt is to take place outdoors, enlist the assistance of neighbors to keep an eye on the children and perhaps even provide hiding places for some of the items.

1 Compile a long list of items to be found. These can range from a pinecone to an old toy doll to a Halloween mask (see list, next page). Just remember that you want the kids to remain safe while hunting (avoid items that would require them to stand on a chair to reach, etc.) and that each item should be available and findable.

2 Divide the children into equal teams, or if you have just a few kids, let each one go on the hunt alone. Give each child a bag for gathering items.

3 Tell the children what their boundaries will be: Can they leave the house or the yard or the block? Be sure they understand that if they leave the designated boundaries, they will be disqualified. Similarly, decide now whether teams must stay together at all times or whether they are allowed to spread out to save time.

4 Line up everyone, bag in hand, so that each child starts out at the same time. Be sure they know you'll be around if they have questions, and instruct them to be back

at your chosen meeting place (usually your home) at a specific time. Each player or team should have a watch or clock so that they can keep track of the time elapsed.

5 Once everyone is back at the meeting place, go through each bag to see what the children have gathered. Add up their points—one point for each item found—and declare the winning player or team.

Keep the Fun Going:

Give the winner(s) the honor of choosing a special treat or picking the next game. Whatever they choose, make sure the losing players get to participate as well. If the winners want to continue the scavenger hunt, let the children make up a list of items for you to find.

List of fun hunt items:

- ★ Shiny rock
- ★ Cotton swab
- ★ Colored leaf
- ★ Checker
- ★ Funky sock
- ★ Treasured DVD
- ★ Playing card
- ★ Piece of fruit
- ★ Hand-written poem from you to your grandchild

Top 5 Ways to Survive a Car Trip

*C*hances are high that at some point you will take your grandkids on a car trip, whether to drive them back to their parents' house or on an excursion to the countryside. If the drive is more than a couple hours long, invest in a portable DVD player and a few of the kids' favorite DVDs. (You can always borrow these from a friend or lending library as well.) Don't feel guilty—your grandkids will be thrilled, and even if they watch two movies, you will still have hours to fill together in the car. Here are a few additional ideas to help pass the spare time before the crankiness begins.

1. **The license-plate or car-number plate game:** Depending on where you live, the children can either search for license plates from all the states and provinces (in the United States and Canada) or try to spot the numbers from 1 to 999 in consecutive order on car number plates (in the United Kingdom and other parts of Europe).

In some countries, you can also search for consecutive alphabet letters on car plates. Some license and number plates, of course, will be harder to find than others. Have the children keep track with a running list. This challenge will give you a chance to talk about geography and which states and countries border one another.

2. Search games: These are the typical I-Spy games you can build around a variety of clues: letters, colors, locations, and so forth. One player begins by saying, "I spy with my little eye something that begins with P," or "something on the ground," or "something red." The first person to guess correctly chooses the next thing to be identified and announces the clue. You can also modify the search as a counting game, in which each child tries to be the first to call out the number of cows, red trucks, green cars, or toll booths she sees. The child who sees the most of any one thing gets to choose the next game.

3. Who Am I?: This is a version of the game 20 Questions. Have one child write down the names of famous people or family members on pieces of paper and place them in a hat or plastic bowl. The people chosen must be well known enough so that everyone in the car will recognize them. The youngest person in the car can be "It" first. She chooses a name out of the hat but does not look at the slip. Everyone else gets a look. "It" has to guess who she is by asking yes and no questions. "Am I male?" "Am I related to you?" "Am I in the movies?" You get the picture. Once she guesses correctly, the game continues with the next youngest player serving as "It."

4. The Age Game: Each participant calls out his or her age. The youngest is the center of attention for the first round: If she is six years old, each player takes a turn saying six things he or she likes about her. It's fine if the contestants repeat things other contestants say. Once you get into the higher double digits, everyone in the car can work as a team to come up with all the things they like about the chosen person. Wouldn't you love to hear the sixty-two things your grandchildren like about you?

5. The Quiet Game: The classic game you should reserve for the end of the trip, when everyone is getting impatient and the noise is driving you crazy. Challenge your grandchildren to be quiet for as long as they can: no talking at all; no grunting; no whining. Anything so much as a whimper will disqualify them. The child who goes the longest without making a sound gets to choose a special treat at your next rest-stop break.

Grandparents' Note

After a long road trip with your grandchildren, consider reading *The Phantom Tollbooth* by Norton Juster. It's the story of a boy who goes on a solo road trip, encounters wordplay and adventure, and learns a few lessons along the way. You will enjoy it as much as your grandchildren do.

Hold Your Own Horse Race

*I*n the United States, the first Saturday in May is renowned among horse enthusiasts as the day of the Kentucky Derby, when the best three-year-old horses race during the "two most exciting minutes in sports." The horses and their jockeys are vying to join the ranks of Regret, Secretariat, Affirmed, Smarty Jones, Barbaro, and many other noble winners. The race is held each year at Churchill Downs in Louisville, Kentucky, but if you haven't scored tickets to the big event, there's no reason that you and the grandkids can't enjoy your own Run for the Roses. All you need to do is design some racing "silks" and conjure up a horse to ride.

1 Have the children choose names for their horses. The Jockey Club, the organization that keeps track of thoroughbreds, requires that a racehorse's name be eighteen characters or fewer, including punctuation and spaces. Other than that restriction, the sky's the limit when it comes to names.

2 Next, have the children design their own jockey silks. Racing silks tend to be colorful, with stripes, polka dots, stars, and other bold designs. Give each child a piece of plain white paper and colorful markers and let them get to work. Carefully secure the papers onto the fronts of their shirts with safety pins.

3 Help the children design their racehorses.

What you will need (for each horse):

- ★ Wooden mop handle or broom stick
- ★ Large white athletic sock
- ★ Sheet of brown felt
- ★ Ball of brown yarn
- ★ Markers in multiple colors
- ★ Liquid glue or hot-glue gun

- ★ Two plastic eyes (optional; can be found at most crafts stores)
- ★ Newspaper or pillow stuffing
- ★ Strong packing tape

1 Gather your materials.

2 Make the horse's head: Stuff the foot of the athletic sock. Pull the elasticized top of the sock over the top of the broom or mop handle and secure it with tape.

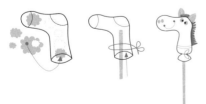

3 Cut the brown felt into ovals to serve as the ears,

then use the remaining felt to create a fringed mane (simply snip fringe along one edge). Glue the felt pieces to the sock using either liquid glue (which will require drying time) or a hot-glue gun (the glue will dry quickly and hold well, but must be used only by an adult). Glue on the eyes, or simply use markers to draw eyes, a mouth, and a nose. Lastly, wind a length of yarn around the horse's "muzzle" and tie a knot, then stretch the yarn down and tie a knot on the outside edge of the stick to form the horse's bridle.

4 Set up the race course. If you have a big backyard, set up the track there—the kids can simply run in a big circle. Otherwise, search out a park or field with sufficient room for the race. Be sure to mark off a clear finish line.

5 Get all the children and their trusty steeds lined up at the starting line. Once you call, "And they're off!" each child will ride his horse around the track. At this point, feel free to put on your best announcer's voice to call the race:

"Secretariat got a little bumped coming out of the gate."

"Affirmed and Alydar are one two as they approach the far turn."

"And Barbaro takes the lead as they turn for home."

Bring along some roses to hand to the winner in the Winner's Circle after the race.

Mint Julep Refresher

What's a Kentucky Derby-style horse race without a Mint Julep? Although you might welcome the Bourbon-laced version, here's a recipe for the alcohol-free variety for the kids.

What you will need:

- ★ About 24 fresh mint leaves
- ★ Two or three cans of cola or tea
- ★ Wedges from one lemon
- ★ Simple syrup (boil two cups water and stir in one cup sugar)
- ★ Ice cubes
- ★ Clear plastic cups and swizzle sticks

Makes 6 cups

1 Place four washed mint leaves in each plastic cup.

2 Cover with cola or tea and a bit of simple syrup. Stir.

3 Add ice cubes and top off the cups with the cola or tea.

4 Add swizzle sticks and lemons for garnish.

Grandparents' Note:

If horses turn out to be a shared interest, watch the big races together. Or rent horse-themed movies like *Dreamer* and read books like *Fritz and the Beautiful Horses* by Jan Brett.

Four-Leaf Clover Hunting

*H*unting four-leaf clovers is an engaging way to spend time outdoors. Just take the grandkids out to the front lawn or nearby park—wherever there might be some promising clover. There's much folklore and history behind the four-leaf clover. Research online together before the excursion. You can learn the words to "I'm Looking over a Four-Leaf Clover" (written in 1927; words by Mort Dixon and lyrics by Harry Words) to get in the mood. Most of all, prepare the kids for the likelihood that you might not find one. (There's only about one four-leafer to every 10,000 three-leaf clovers.)

Equip the kids with a magnifying glass and flashlight to shine extra light on the tiny leaves, as well as a small envelope for protecting their finds. Remember also to bring along a consolation prize in case the hunt comes up empty-handed.

1 Locate the clover patch and assign a spot to each child.

2 Direct the kids to get down on their hands and knees, magnifying glasses in hand, flashlights at the ready, to comb through the clover with their fingers.

3 Once they've exhausted one patch, move on to the next. Make sure to take frequent water breaks and relax from time to time.

4 When a four-leaf clover is found, you and your grandchild are sure to have amazing luck from then on. Once home, protect it with wax paper and press in a heavy book.

Sardines in a Can and Clothespin Tag

*H*ere are a few easy and not-too-competitive games that you can either play with your grandchildren or send them off to play while you make dinner (depending on their ages). Just make sure no dangers are lurking—empty refrigerators or trunks they might hide in, furniture they might pull down on themselves, or things they might bump into. Let them know which rooms are off-limits.

Don't rule out the more traditional versions of these games—hide-and-seek and a good old-fashioned game of tag. They might seem obvious, but sometimes all kids need is a little suggestion to send them off on an afternoon of games.

Sardines in a Can

This version is the opposite of the traditional game of hide-and-seek:

1 One child hides, and the rest of the group splits up to look for him.

2 As each person finds the hider, he or she must get into the hiding place too. (The idea is not to let on that you've found the hider; if you find him while others are around, return to the hiding spot when you're alone.)

3 Ultimately, everyone crams in with the hider until only one child is left looking for the hiding place. That child is now the new hider when the game begins again.

Clothespin Tag

1 Each player starts off with five clothespins clipped to his or her back. The goal is to sneak up on your fellow players and grab a clothespin from *their* backs.

2 When a player successfully grabs another player's clothespin, she kneels down and clips the clothespin to her back. Note: While a player is kneeling to put on the clip *she can't be tagged*. Once she's done, she stands up and reenters the game.

3 The player with the most clothespins wins. But beware: There is never a clear end to the game! Even if one player loses all of his clothespins, he can still try to rebuild his collection. If you need to end the game, give everyone a five-minute warning so they know it's time to wind down.

Play Pirate for a Day

*m*any children go through a phase when they become obsessed with pirate lore and play-acting. Who wouldn't like the idea of escaping on the rough seas and searching for treasure? If your grandchild is going through this stage, there's no better way to while away a rainy day than with some good old-fashioned pirate fun. With a few simple materials, it's easy to create costumes, make a treasure map, and hunt for loot.

Dressing the Part

What you will need:

★ Square of dark felt or black construction paper

★ Hole punch

★ Ball of dark yarn

★ Scarves, bandanas, and vests from your closet

1 Cut the dark felt or black construction paper to form an eye patch.

2 Punch out two small holes and feed the yarn through the holes so that the patch can be secured around the child's head.

3 Pull old vests out of the closet. Anything black and sinister will do. Tie the bandanas and scarves on your heads and knot them into place, pirate-style.

Name That Pirate

At this point, your little pirate is beginning to look the part, but almost as important as looking good is having just the right piratey name to get into the role. Write out ten pirate phrases (e.g., Peg Leg, Ahoy There, Black Beard, Captain, Skull and Bones, Walk the Plank, Shark Tooth, Gunpowder George, One-Eyed Pete, Scurvy Jim, Buccaneer, Jolly Roger, and Mutiny) on small scraps of paper (one name per scrap), then divide the papers evenly in two hats. Have your grandchild choose a piece of paper from each hat to create his pirate name. The combinations will be hilarious. Who can keep a straight face around "Peg Leg Scurvy Jim"? Be sure to get a name for yourself as well.

Making a Treasure Map

What you will need:

★ One teapot of brewed black tea

★ Sheet of white paper

★ Colored marker

1 Brew some strong black tea and let it cool.

2 Lay down some newspaper on your kitchen counter to protect against spills.

3 Have your grandchild rip the edges off the sheet of white paper, dip the paper in the cooled tea, and crinkle it to make it look old and used.

4 Help squeeze out the excess tea, then straighten out the sheet and allow it to dry.

5 Once the paper is dry, draw a map to imagined buried treasure using made-up clues and an illustrated compass. This "aged" document will have an instant old-fashioned, piratey look—the perfect souvenir from a very fun day!

Hunting for Treasure

Making a pretend treasure map will get your grandchild in the mood to hunt for loot. A simple hunt is easy to concoct.

1 Use the castoff pirate-name slips to write your clues. Keep the instructions to simple locations your grandchild can easily figure out: Where is the ship's galley where we eat our pirate grub? (The kitchen.) Where does a pirate make waves? (The bathtub.) Where does a pirate recharge his battery? (His bed.) If your grandchild is too young to read, simply draw a picture and keep it as uncomplicated as you can.

2 Hand the child the first clue, and then place the next clue in the spot where the first clue leads him. Keep two or three clues ahead of your pirate at all times.

3 If your grandchild is old enough to read, you should write the last clue in code: Simply come up with an easy substitution code (for example, each letter of the alphabet corresponds to another symbol, where A is 4 or G is white) and write out the key to the code. Now write the clue in code, and leave the clue and the decoder key where the child will find it (the location of the next-to-last clue).

4 Make sure to have real treasure waiting at the end of the hunt—a few shiny quarters, fruit rollups, or a pint of ice-cream in a mini-cooler will do the trick.

Make Your Own Grog!

What pirate adventure would be complete without a little grog? Traditionally, grog was simply water with a bit of rum mixed in, a dash of lime to prevent scurvy, and a few spoonfuls of cane sugar to cut the bitterness, but you can come up with your own child-friendly concoction: Mix six cups cold water, a cup of lime juice (or the juice from 6 or 7 limes), and one cup white sugar for a good old-fashioned Jolly Roger limeade!

Plant Fairy and Goblin Gardens

*C*hildren love the idea of magical places conjured in books and films, but the very best flights of imagination are those that start with the kids themselves. As a grandparent, you are the perfect partner for letting their imaginations run wild, and creating a "real" fairy or goblin garden provides the perfect project for you to plan and work on together. These gardens are essentially miniature worlds inhabited by fantastical creatures that come to life in the child's mind and imagination but take their real-world forms in your own backyard or garden. They can be as elaborate or as simple as your grandchild chooses.

Girls tend toward the fairy-garden concept and boys to the goblins, but of course there are no rules. Whatever your grandchild chooses, research together to uncover the traditions and folklore behind these creatures. For example, there are many books about flower fairies and what draws them to a garden. (Hint: Lavender is an excellent lure.) But you and your grandchild may decide that a cranberry fairy would like red leaves, a ladybug fairy might like leaves with spots, or a cherry tree fairy might like all things pink. For the goblin garden, your grandchild might choose to focus on dark, scary-looking plants, plants with spiky leaves, or plants that have the word *wizard* in their names.

The garden can take its form either in a large pot or a small portion of your yard. Using a pot means the child will have the option of taking it home and continuing to care for it, whereas making the garden a permanent part of your home landscape gives the child something to look forward to for his or her next visit. Fairies bring magic and goblins bring mischief—so plan accordingly.

Grandparents' Note:

There are entire Web sites dedicated to fairy gardens, with specific directions and fancy props for purchase. That's fine if you want a professional look, but a homemade garden will draw as much magic and mischief as an expensive, planned one.

If you can dedicate a portion of your garden to this project, choose a section measuring two square feet or larger. If using a pot, choose one with sufficient room for props: a two-foot-long container would work well, or a circular pot measuring at least two feet in circumference.

What you will need:

* Medium to large sturdy pot or a small plot of soil
* Small plantings
* Container mix (if using a pot)
* Trowel
* Glitter, dried flowers, and herbs for fairy or goblin "dust"
* Props (see below)

1 The props are where the fun begins. If possible, take a trip to a crafts, hardware, or pet store to find materials to make structures for the fairies and goblins to hide within. (Alternatively, simply rummage around your old storage drawers and basement for materials.) You can use anything from painted rocks and shells and plastic jewels to bridges and small huts designed for fish tanks. Your grandchild can also use sticks and glue to make structures or small plastic dishes for ponds or streams. Just remember that whatever you use will be exposed to the rain and cold, so the materials should by durable.

2 Take a moment together to sketch the garden on paper. Where will the fairy's bed be? Where can the goblin hide? Where should the flowers be planted?

3 Dedicate an afternoon to gluing, building, and painting the props and other structures so that they have time to dry, if necessary.

4 Now carefully plant the flowers and other plantings according to the sketch.

5 Anchor the bridges and shells and other structures securely into the dirt.

6 Finally, liberally sprinkle the garden with fairy or goblin dust, and you're ready for the magic to take hold.

Hold a Spring-Cleaning Yard Sale

*Y*ou might not realize it in the early months of grandparenting—perhaps not until your grandchildren are walking and talking—but some of the best activities you can do together involve things as mundane as rummaging through old clothes and linen closets. The great benefit of these sorts of adventures is that they're fun *and* they give you the satisfaction of completing a long-neglected cleaning task. Present the activity with two extra fun goals in mind: Tell your grandchildren to think of it as a treasure hunt as you pick through items you haven't used in years, and put everything you don't want in a pile for a yard sale later that day.

1 Let your grandchildren choose the closet they find the most interesting. The closet full of family photos, old report cards, and letters? The linen closet that's chockfull of your own children's old toys and puzzles?

2 Tell your grandchildren you want to see everything before a final decision is made; then designate piles for keeping, selling, and trash. Each grandchild will be allowed to keep one or more items,

depending on what you think is fair, for an extra incentive.

3 Take the time to recount the backstories of the more interesting items you come across. The towel you bought (or accidentally packed in your suitcase) on your honeymoon. The jacket you wore for your fortieth wedding anniversary party.

4 Once the closet is empty and you've organized the piles, ask your grandchildren to explain why they chose

particular items for the "save" pile, then tell them about the objects' history. Carefully put the rest of the items to be saved neatly back in the closet.

5 Go through the items meant for the trash to make sure there's nothing worth salvaging for donation or for making a crazy quilt (see page 99). Place the rest in a plastic bag for trash day.

6 Now that you're left with only the "sale" pile, find blank stickers or scrap paper to price each item. Let the kids tell you what they think each object is worth. This is a good opportunity to talk about money and inflation, especially if you remember what you originally paid and know what the item costs new today.

7 Set up a table outside your home and let your grandchildren make a poster to advertise the sale. They can help with customer purchases.

8 At the end of the day, have your grandchildren decide what to do with the money from the yard sale. Perhaps they'd like to get a special treat or to donate the proceeds to a charitable organization.

9 Donate the items that you don't sell.

Grandparents' Note

Commit to the task! Do *not* stop halfway through, with piles outside and inside the closet. If your grandchildren get antsy, take a break and have a snack. But then come back to the project. It will be satisfying for everyone to see it through from start to finish.

Hold a Mock Election

*y*our grandchildren might be learning about voting in school, but you have probably voted in enough elections in your lifetime that you can tell them things they'll never read in a book. Take the opportunity to relate the first time you voted: Who were the candidates? What was going on in the world? What do you consider to be the most important election? Is there one vote you would go back and change if you had the chance? What about during your parents' lifetime? Were there restrictions on women or black citizens voting when they were young adults?

To bring the process to the real world, stage a mock election. Create two imaginary candidates who will each stand for different sides of an argument that your grandchildren will immediately grasp: Candidate A can stand for chocolate chip cookies being better than brownies. Perhaps Candidate B is running on the claim that apples are better than oranges. This activity works best with at least five children participating. You don't want a deadlocked election!

What you will need:

* ★ Poster board
* ★ Markers
* ★ Slips of paper to serve as ballots (one for each voter)
* ★ Pencils (one for each voter)

1 Let each child choose which candidate to support.

2 Take time to talk about how candidates campaign. Decide for yourself whether you want to discuss negative ads—it could add some fun ("Don't vote for Candidate B—she'll make you eat an apple a day!").

3 Let the children use the poster board and markers to make campaign signs with slogans: Candidate B: "Vote for Me. I'll Keep the Doctor Away." Candidate A: "You'll Have a Richer Future If You Vote for Me."

4 See if your grandchildren can come up with a few good arguments why their candidate is the best. If they're old enough to grasp the concept, let them hold a mini mock debate, with you serving as moderator.

5 Talk about the benefits and drawbacks of secret balloting versus voting with a show of hands. If the group is in favor of balloting, have them write the names of both candidates on slips of paper (one ballot per voter), with an empty box next to each name. If your grandchildren are too young to write, they can simply draw pictures of the candidates.

6 Distribute the ballots to each young voter and give each a pencil to mark his or her choice. Have them fold their ballots in half and place them in a bowl or hat.

7 As the neutral poll worker, you will count the votes and announce the winner.

8 Hold a victory party. If Candidate A wins, bake up a nice batch of chocolate chip cookies. If Candidate B prevails, make apple muffins or an apple pie, or serve apple slices as a snack.

Take a Trip to the Toy Store

*D*edicated grandparent that you are, you're probably the sort who volunteers to watch the grandkids when your son and daughter-in-law take a special trip without the children. But as Day 3 rolls around, you've already been to the museum, the local diner, the park, the nature center, the library, the arcade, and an indoor playground. It rained yesterday so you let them watch a few videos—and when you woke up this morning, it was *still* raining. What to do? It might sound extravagant, but consider taking the children to the toy store for a little excursion. Not only will it be thrilling for the kids and get you out of the house, but it'll also give them something new to play with when you return home. Just remember to set a few ground rules.

* Emphasize that this outing is special and not something you'll do every time they visit.
* Tell them they can each choose only one thing.
* Set a clear price limit. If you say $10–$15, they will each be able to choose a small building-block kit, puzzle, or art kit. In the end, it won't cost you much more than a trip to the movies.
* Let them take their time browsing the store; it is, after all, a desperate attempt to get out of the house and pass some time.
* Bring along a pad of paper and pencil. If your grandchildren see more than they are allowed to purchase that day or have a hard time deciding, you can start an official birthday or holiday gift list.
* Once home, let them play with their new toys while you get in a little "me" time reading the paper or a good book. If one child chose a board game, play together to pass the rainy afternoon.

Grandparent Wisdom

WHAT ARE YOUR FAVORITE MEMORIES OF ACTIVITIES YOU'VE SHARED WITH YOUR GRANDCHILDREN?

❝ I was reading a story to my oldest grandson—he was about five. I got up for a minute, came back, sat down, and he started to read the story to me. [Another time] I was walking back from the beach with my oldest grandson. It was my birthday, and he gave me a seashell for a present. I still have it.

I also loved tea parties with my granddaughter. They went from picnics on the kitchen floor to elaborate colonial tea parties with American Girl dolls, with minuet music and fancy sandwiches. Just the two of us.❞

—Lois, grandmother of 6

❝ At Wildwood: the beach and the various rides. [I was] looking at the gleam in their eyes, their big radiant smiles, and enjoying how they yelled, "Pop-pop, Pop-pop!" Playing in the sand, running to the water's edge, the joy of watching the kids having fun—it was their first time at the beach!❞

—Victor, grandfather of 3

❝ Taking them fishing, and baking cookies.❞

—Bonnie, grandmother of 3

❝ Planting and growing a garden together, and harvesting and eating the vegetables.❞

—Judy, grandmother of 4

Crafts and Cooking

By the time you get to be a grandparent, you've no doubt developed a whole world of interests, favorite pastimes, and cherished memories. You are now poised to pass on those experiences to a new generation. There is simply no better way to bond with your grandchildren than to sit side-by-side and create new experiences together, whether by baking a cherished family cookie recipe, sewing a crazy quilt, or uncovering long-forgotten family photographs and mementos.

In this chapter, you will discover or rediscover recipes, crafts, and projects that give your grandchildren the hands-on experience and satisfaction of creating, whether it's preserving a moment in time with a diorama, picking apples for the best fruit cobbler imaginable, or compiling a picture dictionary to learn a new language together. You will experience the profound pleasure of seeing their small hands working alongside your own, mixing dough, creating family keepsakes, and building new memories.

You and the children are poised at the intersection of multiple generations, and as you spend time together—perhaps even comparing notes about events from your childhood and theirs—you are imparting lessons about traditions, history, and life that they will carry with them into the future.

Sugar Fixes: Foolproof Cookie Recipes

*C*hances are, your grandchildren already associate visits to your house with some delectable cookie treat—and it's your grandparental duty to provide the sugary indulgences they usually don't get at home. What's your signature cookie recipe? Perhaps it's the holiday treat you make for family gatherings, or one that's been passed down from generation to generation. For the perfect rainy-day or preholiday activity, allow them to help you mix and bake their favorite cookies. One child can add the dry ingredients while another mixes them in the bowl, and everyone can take turns cutting out favorite cookie shapes. The recipes that follow were gathered from different sides of our family.

Nanny's Butter Biscuits

* 1 lb. granulated sugar
* ½ lb. lightly salted butter, softened
* 4 eggs
* 4 tsp. baking powder
* 4 cups flour

Makes 3 to 4 dozen (depending on cookie-cutter size)

1 Preheat oven to 375°F.

2 Cream together sugar and butter in a large mixing bowl.

3 Add eggs one at a time, using a sturdy spoon to mix.

4 Add baking powder and flour.

5 Form dough into two balls and cover with plastic wrap. Refrigerate overnight.

6 When you're ready to make the cookies, sprinkle additional flour mixed with sugar on wax paper and on top of dough. Roll out dough on wax paper, using a rolling pin.

7 Cut out shapes using your favorite cookie cutters. Use your hands or a spatula to gently transfer cookies to baking sheets lined with parchment paper.

8 Bake 8–10 minutes. Let cool before transferring to an airtight container.

Florence's Butter Cookies

★ ½ lb. lightly salted butter, softened

★ ⅔ cup sugar

★ 1 egg

★ 1 tsp. vanilla

★ 2 cups plus ¼ cup flour

★ ½ tsp. baking powder

Makes about 2 dozen

1 Preheat oven to 350°F.

2 With clean hands or a hand mixer, blend butter and sugar in a large mixing bowl.

3 Add egg and vanilla, mixing with a sturdy spoon.

4 Add remaining dry ingredients slowly and mix until the batter forms a moist dough.

5 Spoon 1 tsp. of batter at a time onto ungreased cookie sheets.

6 Flatten with fork tines or the lightly greased bottom of a small glass.

7 Bake 15–20 minutes or until edges are golden brown.

8 Let cool before transferring to an airtight container.

Grandparents' Note

Next time your grandchildren visit for a holiday weekend, why not put together a book of favorite cookie recipes from extended family members, friends, and neighbors? Include the cookies' special history and the stories behind them.

Sew a Family Crazy Quilt

*U*nless you're one of those rare people who throws things away when you no longer need them, you probably have a good stash of clothes and blankets that haven't been touched in years but are too precious to discard. Fabrics have histories: the dress you wore to get married in 45 years ago; the blouse your sister wore when she eloped, the baby blanket that was handed down from generation to generation but is now too frayed to give to a baby. These can provide great material for wonderful crafts and sewing activities with your grandchildren.

A crazy quilt is a patchwork quilt without design, making it the perfect sort of craft to do with small children. There are no wrong answers when it comes to making a crazy quilt. Typically, they are made up of diverse pieces of fabric that are sewn onto a larger cloth foundation. The finished pieces will become family heirlooms, bringing the past and the present together. They make great gifts, and they will always be full of stories. Let the grandkids rummage through your pile of old fabrics, feeling the different textures. Take your time and share the history of your favorite pieces. And then get to work!

Crazy Quilt History

The crazy quilt became popular during the Victorian era, when upper-class women spent much of their leisure time doing needlework. Oriental designs, which were popular during that time, are thought to have influenced the characteristic ornate styles and designs of the quilts, which became fixtures in homes.

1 Choose a foundation fabric. You can buy something at a fabric store or simply use your sharp scissors to cut an old white sheet into whatever shape you want your quilt to be. Take into consideration how much fabric you have to work with and what you might use the final creation for (a pillow? a wall hanging? an actual quilt?).

2 Let your grandchildren choose 10–20 bits of fabric (or more, if making a bigger piece) to use in their quilts.

3 Cut the fabric they've selected into the different shapes they choose: circles, squares, hearts, stars, horseshoes, moons, and so on.

4 If your grandchildren are old enough to use needle and thread, allow them to sew the fabric to the foundation piece. Otherwise, have the children glue the bits of fabric—you can sew them on later if you wish. Let the children decide where to place the pieces. Don't feel you have to fill the foundation—white or whatever color the fabric is can show through. It's their design, and it can be anything they want it to be!

Backstitch Basics

This is a great opportunity to teach the children the basics of backstitching.

1 Thread the needle with 24 inches or so of thread and knot the double end. The key here is to make the length of thread easy enough for the children to manage without having to rethread over and over again.

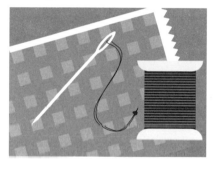

2 Show the children how to push the needle through the front of the patch fabric and the foundation.

3 Next, show them how to move the thread about an eighth of an inch over the piece

and push the needle the other way through the back of the patch and foundation.

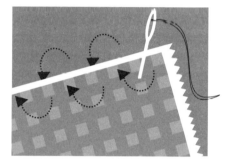

4 Pull the needle through the back of the foundation fabric.

5 Continue to sew, allowing the children to try pushing the needle through the front and then back and then front again, until you have either finished sewing the piece or the thread has run out.

6 Finish the stitch at the back of the quilt, leaving enough thread to tie a knot. Cut the thread at the needle, and tie off a good knot.

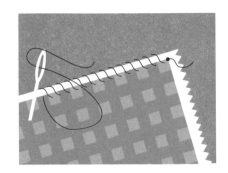

The Scoop: Creating a Family Newspaper

*I*n the age of e-mail, Internet, and webcams, keeping up with the latest family news usually is just a click away. But these don't provide the permanent delights of creating family history the old-fashioned way: in a printed newspaper your grandchildren can touch and feel and send to relatives near and far. There's no better way to share old and new family stories.

What you will need:

★ Pencils and paper

★ Tape or glue

★ Scissors

★ Computer (if you have one)

★ Telephone

★ Photo scanner (optional)

1 Have your grandchild compile a list of family members to interview (great-uncles, aunts, cousins, other grandparents), complete with each interviewee's phone number, e-mail address, and snail-mail address.

2 With your grandchild, compile a list of interview questions:

- Is someone expecting a new baby?
- Are there any marriages on the horizon?
- Did anyone in the family immigrate to the United States? If so, from which country?
- Did someone begin a business years ago?
- Who are (and were) the family pets?
- What was the best family vacation ever? the grandest family gathering? the most looked-forward-to family holiday?

3 Help your grandchild contact each interviewee by phone, by e-mail, or in person, then have her conduct the interview, taking notes along the way (or simply printing out the e-mailed replies).

4 Help write up the stories. If she's too young to write long entries, have her dictate to you what she remembers from the conversations and then let her draw pictures showing the main aspects of the story. If she's old enough to use the computer herself, let her type up each story. If you don't have a computer, you can use a typewriter or simply write the stories longhand.

5 Now bring out your photo albums and allow her to choose pictures that best illustrate the stories. She can then either scan the photos or tape the originals to her "master" layout pages.

6 Once the paper is finished, make copies: Either print out multiple copies on your home printer or take them to a local print shop or library for photocopying.

7 Create a master list of all the recipients. This is an excellent time for your grandchild to learn who is related to whom and where each group of relatives lives. Have her address the envelopes and mail the copies.

Grandparents' Note

If you have more than one grandchild visiting at one time, have each one do a job—reporter, writer, illustrator, editor—that best suits his or her age.

Fruit Picking and the Secrets to Amazing Cobbler

*T*aking your grandchild on an excursion to a pick-your-own farm or farmers market can be a full day's activity. There's nothing better than enjoying fresh local berries, peaches, and apples, and some farms even offer hayrides and soft-serve ice cream in whatever flavor of fruit grows in the fields. For grandchildren who live in a different growing region from yours, this will also be an opportunity to enjoy fruits at their source and to discuss the environmental importance of choosing local foods. Be aware that picking fruit can take hours. Don't forget to plan ahead with enough bottled water and bathroom breaks!

Once you've all eaten your fill of whole fruit, you have many options for creating pies, jams, scones, and pancakes. The following cobbler recipe, however, is a crowd-pleasing favorite. It calls for peaches, but cherries, blueberries, blackberries, and apples can also be used, and it's especially child-friendly: Little hands can carefully wash fruit, pull stems off berries, and whisk the batter. Older children can melt the butter and stir the cooking fruit.

When the golden-brown dessert emerges from the oven, it's like magic: The fruit will have moved to the bottom, and the cake has floated to the top. Serve the cobbler with plenty of vanilla ice cream.

Cobbler

There are loads of cobbler recipes out there. This one is based on a show-stopper from the book *Smokestack Lightening: Adventures in the Heart of Barbecue Country*, by Lolis Eric Elie, which we've customized to suit the tastes of our family.

What you will need:

- ★ ¼ lb. (one stick) melted butter
- ★ 4 or 5 cups peaches, washed and sliced
- ★ At least 1½ cups sugar
- ★ 1 teaspoon cinnamon
- ★ ¼ teaspoon ground nutmeg
- ★ 1 cup flour
- ★ 2 teaspoons baking powder
- ★ ¼ tsp. salt
- ★ 1 cup milk

Serves 8

1 Preheat oven to 350°F.

2 Butter and flour a 9-by-13-inch glass casserole dish. Pour in melted butter.

3 In a saucepan, slowly cook the fruit with ½ cup sugar until soft. Add cinnamon and nutmeg. The fruit should be sweet, so add more sugar as necessary.

4 In a separate bowl, combine flour with 1 cup sugar, baking powder, and salt. Whisk in milk and pour mixture into the pan over the butter.

5 Gently spoon cooked fruit evenly over batter.

6 Bake about 45 minutes or until golden brown.

Create Your Own Ice-Cream Cake

*m*ost kids love ice-cream cake, but it's usually reserved for special occasions. As a grandparent, you can change all that. Even better than presenting a store-bought cake when your young guest arrives, indulge in a delectable make-your-own cake project. Here's a fool-proof, little-mess method for making this delicious and cool confection

What you will need:

* ★ 27–30 vanilla ice-cream sandwiches
* ★ 2–3 tubs (8 ounces) whipped nondairy topping
* ★ Sprinkles (rainbow and/ or chocolate)
* ★ Chocolate sauce, small candies, chocolate chips, maraschino cherries, and other toppings

1 Line the bottom of a 9-by-13-inch glass pan with one layer of ice-cream sandwiches.

2 Spread a layer of whipped topping over the sandwiches.

3 Place another layer of ice-cream sandwiches over the whipped topping, and then another layer of whipped topping. Spread this last layer as smoothly as possible since it'll be the top of the cake.

4 Decorate with sprinkles. You can also drizzle a small amount of chocolate sauce to make a design or add M&M-type candies or other toppings. Adding cherries will turn it into an ice-cream sundae cake!

5 Place the cake in the freezer for at least an hour to let the ingredients solidify.

6 Remove from freezer, cut, eat, and enjoy!

The Secrets to Delicious Homemade Pickles

*C*rispy, sour, salty, or sweet, pickles are a taste sensation. Whether you grew up with the store-bought variety or had a pickling recipe your parents handed down to you, there's no better way to pass the time than by having your grandkids assist in transforming lowly cucumbers into tasty pickles. It's a great activity for an overnight or multiple-day visit. If it's a short weekend visit, the overnight recipe is the way to go. If you have a week together, choose the recipe that requires three days of pickling. The pickles will probably be a bit more sour-tasting, which many kids prefer.

Grandparents' Note

If you have your own garden, you can send your grandkids a progress report "from the field" in anticipation of their next visit. If you time things just right, they can help harvest the crop for pickling. This is a great way to have them enjoy a time-honored tradition of preserving fresh vegetables for the long haul.

Overnight Pickles

* ★ 2 cups water
* ★ 2 tbsp. kosher salt
* ★ 1 cup vinegar
* ★ 2 lbs. cucumbers (smaller, Kirby-style work best)
* ★ 3 or 4 cloves garlic
* ★ handful fresh dill weed

1 In a large pot, bring the water, salt, and vinegar to a boil and let it simmer as you prepare the cucumbers.

2 Wash the cucumbers and cut them into halves lengthwise.

3 Place the cut cucumbers in a large bowl. Add garlic and dill, then pour the vinegar mixture over the cucumbers.

4 Let the cucumbers cool to room temperature, then cover and refrigerate them overnight.

Three-Day Pickles

Properly canned pickles may be stored indefinitely, but they should be good for eating after three days.

* ★ 6 cups water
* ★ ½ cup kosher salt
* ★ ¼ cup vinegar
* ★ 5 pounds cucumbers
* ★ 7–12 whole cloves garlic
* ★ Small head fresh dill
* ★ ½ tsp. mustard seed
* ★ Bay leaf (1 leaf for each jar)
* ★ Red pepper flakes to taste

1 In a large pot, bring the water, salt, and vinegar to a boil and let it simmer as you prepare the cucumbers.

2 Wash the cucumbers and remove blossom ends.

3 Place the cucumbers in a large bowl.

4 Pour the vinegar mixture over the cucumbers.

5 Pack cucumbers into sterilized jars, leaving about ¼ inch of space at top.

6 Add equal amounts of garlic, dill, mustard seed, bay leaf, and pepper flakes to each jar.

7 Pour remaining liquid into each jar, leaving ¼ inch of head space.

8 Cap each jar with tightly fitted lid.

9 Place filled jars in actively boiling water in a canner or pressure cooker for 15 minutes.

Important Note

Booouoo of all the boiling involved in canning and pickling, this activity should be done only under close supervision. If you have concerns about improperly canning your pickled cucumbers, consult the U.S.D.A.'s Web site for specific instructions and precautions.

Fun and Games with the Family Photo Album

*O*nce your grandkids are old enough to comprehend that, believe it or not, Mom and Dad and Grandma and Grandpa were once babies, too, there's no better way to introduce them to the pleasures of perusing the family album. The thrill of seeing their own baby pictures will be second only to seeing their *parents'* baby snaps. Go through random pictures on a rainy day, or pull out that box of unorganized snapshots after a busy day at the zoo as a way to wind down before dinner. Let your grand-children choose one photo to take with them. They're certain to cherish it always.

Creating games around organizing the photos will also lead to endless opportunities for story-telling and remembrance. The photos can be put into chronological order, or you can play a guessing game by asking the kids to identify who is in the photo. Some ideas for activities follow.

Play the Photo Memory Game

1 Make two sets of color copies of 10 or 20 photos (or any other number, as long as it's even).

2 Trim the individual images to photo size.

3 Mix them up, then place the photos facedown on the ground or on a table, in symmetrical rows.

4 Have each grandchild turn over two photos at a time, trying to find a match. If a match isn't found, the pictures should be placed facedown again in their spots, and the next player turns over two more.

5 The goal of the game is to remember where each photo is placed and to turn over more pairs than any other player. Whoever ends up with the most matches, wins!

Photo Puzzles

Kids love completing jigsaw puzzles, so why not add another dimension to this activity by creating puzzles from family photographs?

1 Using your home computer scanner or local copy center, enlarge a few family photos to about 8 by10 inches, and print them out.

2 Glue the enlarged photos to individual pieces of cardboard, and let them dry.

3 Once the mountings are dry, trim any excess white border from the photos and cut them into shapes. Any shape will do, but keep the number to no more than 10 pieces for children under four and no more than 20 for children under six.

4 If you are using more than one photo, be sure to place the pieces to each puzzle separately, in a plastic storage bag.

5 Now let your grandchildren try to piece together the original photos. (Hint: Keep the original photo nearby just in case you forget how the pieces go together!)

Collections and Crafting with Collections

*n*ow that you're a grandparent, it's a great time to pull out your old stamp or bottle-cap collection and go through it with your grandchild—or to choose something that you are both interested in and begin collecting together. Think of the excitement of showing your grandchild the rock you found for your collection while visiting a volcano in Hawaii, or the thrill he'll have when he shows you the Petoskey stone he found while traveling with his parents in northern Michigan. You may ultimately decide to pass along your treasured stamp collection to your grandchild as a way to kindle the same excitement you felt when you started collecting as a child.

Here are some collecting ideas, along with craft suggestions.

Buttons

Many believe that buttons were invented in ancient Egypt and Greece as purely decorative items: they became more functional as time went on. As you and your grandchild build a collection, read up on the history of this marvelously simple device. You'll find that during the Middle Ages, men's buttons (unlike women's) were presumably shifted to the left side of garments so a man could quickly unbutton his coat with his left hand while drawing his sword with his right. Buttons can be made of gold, glass, fabric, brass, china, wood, plastic, ivory, tortoiseshell, and even diamonds. Some are plain; others have pictures and designs.

1 Begin by going through your drawers and other storage areas with your grandchild in search of loose buttons. Look at old garments in the closet to see whether there are unusual examples to add to the collection.

2 Instruct your grandchild to search for buttons in the same way at his home (remind him not to pull buttons off clothes without permission, of course) and to be on the lookout for buttons in second-hand and thrift stores.

3 Designate a jar for storing the buttons you each collect during your times together and apart. Later, you can sort them and affix them to category cards (with thread or glue) according to color, material, or the type of garment the button came from.

4 Alternatively, you can simply use the buttons for crafting—the ultimate way to recycle materials and make some beautiful homemade gifts:

- Decorate a pillow or make a collage with the buttons.
- Glue or sew colorful buttons on paper plates, then string together three or four plates to make a wall hanging.
- Thread buttons together to make a necklace, bracelet, or belt.
- Glue buttons to a box to make a jewelry or keepsake box.

Bottle Caps

Collecting metal beverage caps will get your grandchild excited every time you open a bottle. Plus, bottle caps are items you can easily bring back from trips as souvenirs for your grandchild.

1 Start by collecting them in a bowl, jar, or plastic bag. Your grandchild will like the way they jingle.

2 Sort the caps by type or color, or just pile them together and see how high of a tower you can build. Make groups of 5, 10, or 25 as a fun counting exercise.

3 Once you've collected at least 100 caps, create a bottle-cap collage:

- Help your grandchild flatten half of the caps with a hammer. Be careful not to hurt any little (or big!) fingers. Leave the others as is.
- Paint a stiff piece of cardboard with a color of your grandchild's choosing.
- Once the paint is dry, glue on the bottle caps. Use strong white glue or, if you have one, a hot-glue gun. (Remember to keep it away from small children.)
- Arrange the bottle caps randomly or in a design. Glue the unflattened caps face out so their insides show.
- Once the glue is dry, secure a heavy piece of string to the back so that the collage may be hung on the wall.

Stamps

Serious stamp collecting requires investments of time and resources. Perhaps you already have a collection from when you first started collecting that you can now share with your grandchild. Alternatively, you might want to take some of the seriousness out of the endeavor by collecting everyday stamps that have already been used and cancelled. They won't be as valuable as unused stamps, but they will be easier to come by and you can always use them for craft projects at a later time.

Carefully cut the stamps you like from the envelopes and collect them in a bag or binder; have your grandchild do the same. When you talk on the phone, you can tell each other about the stamps you've found. Once you and your grandchild have collected a good quantity, you can create personalized "stamp stationery" that only you and the child can use.

1 Buy blank white cards with envelopes at a crafts store.

2 Cover the front of the card with glue and affix any number of stamps in a design of your choosing. You can make patterns or random designs, or you can sort and glue by color or shade.

3 Let the cards dry completely before pairing them with the envelopes.

4 Reserve the stationery only for correspondence with your grandchild. You can send your grandchild notes on the cards you make, and your grandchild can do the same with his. If your grandchild is too young to write, he can simply draw pictures on the stationery. (Make sure you address and stamp the letters for him so all he has to do is get Mom or Dad to walk him to the mailbox.)

Rocks and Shells

Depending on where you and your grandchild live, you likely have an abundance of either shells or rocks suitable for building a collaborative collection. Discuss whether you want to collect one or the other (or both). Take some time and look around to see what you can gather.

After a storm or during low tide are both good times to hunt for shells on the beach. Bring along a plastic bucket or bag to carry your finds. Remind your grandchild of the ground rules: If you notice a living animal inside the shell, let it be. Don't disturb a clam or a mussel who is just minding his own business. If the shell is empty, it's fair game.

Rocks can be found almost everywhere—in fields, along dirt roads, in the woods, and in streams. Some rocks will be native to the region; others will stand out because of their distinctive shapes and colors. Be selective of the rocks you take home—they're very heavy once you load several of them into your backpack or bucket.

Once you have your rocks and shells at home, wash them carefully with soap and water. Place them in empty egg cartons, adding notes of where you found each one and when. (Some hobby shops also sell plastic boxes that can serve this purpose.) You and your grandchild can check out rock- or shell-collecting books from the library and identify your finds in greater detail.

Alternatively—and especially if you're collecting with an eye toward making crafts rather than a science project—choose big, smooth rocks to serve as paperweights: Simply paint a design and cover it with shellac once the paint has dried. Tiny, colorful rocks may be wired together to make beautiful jewelry. Certain types of rocks and shells might be glued together to make figures.

Discover a New Language by Compiling a Picture Dictionary

A picture dictionary is simply a small book that teaches children alphabet letters and words through pictures and illustrations. You and your grandchildren can take this idea one step further by creating a visual dictionary in a new language—one that reflects your family's heritage or simply one that you or your grandchild know well or have always wanted to learn.

Whether your mother tongue was Spanish or your grandchild has dreams of visiting Mexico, France, or Israel, research the source materials that will provide the alphabet letters and words the two of you will need to create the book. Obviously, the alphabet you use will depend on the language to be translated, so gather the right resources to determine the letters' proper shapes and sequence.

What you will need:

★ Paper (at least one page per letter of the alphabet plus a front and back cover)

★ Colorful markers

★ Foreign-language dictionary

★ Hole punch

★ Small roll of ribbon

1 Take some time to talk about the language. Was it ever a big part of your life? How? Are there foreign words you say that might already be familiar to your grandchild?

2 Review the alphabet in order, one letter at a time. For example, a Hebrew visual dictionary will start with the letter "aleph"; a Greek dictionary will start with "alpha";

a Spanish dictionary will begin with the letter "A."

3 Dedicate one page for each letter and illustration, then choose a word that begins with the letter. For example, your grandchild may choose the word *apple* to begin the book with the letter *A*. Have her translate *apple* into Spanish, French, or whatever language you are using, then write both the English version and the foreign-language version in big letters at the top of the page.

4 Have your grandchild draw a picture of the word.

5 Continue through the alphabet, one letter at a time. There's no need to rush the process: This might be a project you do over days or weeks instead of a single afternoon.

6 Once the alphabet is complete, collect all the pages in order and punch three holes along the left side of each, making sure not to cut off any of the pictures or words.

7 Have your grandchild create a cover for the book (be sure to include the authors' names) and punch holes that correspond to the interior pages' holes.

8 Cut three short pieces of ribbon and tie each piece into a hole, leaving enough slack so that the pages turn easily.

Make a Holiday
Dinner Centerpiece

*E*ven though holiday family gatherings are always highly anticipated, they can be surprisingly long days for your grandchildren to endure. Sure, there are relatives around, but many stores and attractions are closed, and everyone is left sitting around indoors while the grown-ups cook the meal. You need a project the kids can dig into. Help your grandchildren make a festive centerpiece for the table. In the end, they'll remember the time you spent together far longer than they will remember the food. Holidays are about traditions, after all, and you might just have started one of your own!

This activity is meant to be spontaneous, so most of your supplies should be readily at hand in and around your home.

1 Dig out a nice-sized basket from an old floral arrangement, a long-unused Easter basket, or even the bread basket you use at dinnertime. If you're at a loss, simply pick out a large wooden bowl.

2 Equip the children with plastic bags and take them outside. They will be happy to escape the strong food smells, overheated house, and overly excited adults.

3 Direct the children to gather items for the basket: colorful autumn or bright green spring leaves and branches, pine cones, pretty rocks, wild flowers, and so forth.

4 Once the children have had the chance to blow off some steam outdoors, bring them back in to search around the house for fruit, decorative accents (feathers and beads), or even toys that might be fun and colorful.

5 Lay out all of the items on a table so you can all assess your finds. Rinse and dry anything that needs to be cleaned. Next, help the children place each object in a pleasing arrangement in the basket.

6 Cut out shapes and confetti from the brightly colored construction paper. Place and/or sprinkle the paper throughout the arrangement to connect the pieces visually.

7 Finally, tie a length of ribbon around the entire basket, and place the arrangement at the center of the table. Voilà!

Bring On the Bead People

*C*reating beaded characters is an activity you and your grandchildren can do for hours. Make them as gifts or create an entire village of bead people for endless fun! Supplies are easy to obtain at traditional crafts stores. Show the children how to make one or two figures, then let them try their hands at it.

What you will need (for one bead person):

- ★ 2 pipe cleaners
- ★ 3 plastic pony beads (colorful beads with holes that fit the pipe cleaner)
- ★ 24 triangular plastic beads (beads with three rounded points)
- ★ 4 plastic snowflake beads (colorful beads with 6 points)
- ★ 1 metal keychain ring
- ★ 1 large wooden bead (about two or three times larger than the pony beads)
- ★ Paint or stickers
- ★ Short lengths of yarn
- ★ Glue

1 Gather your supplies.

2 Insert one pipe cleaner through the keychain ring, positioning the ring in the middle of the cleaner, then fold cleaner in half.

3 Push both ends of the pipe cleaner through the large wooden bead, positioning it just under the keychain ring. (The wooden bead will serve as the head.)

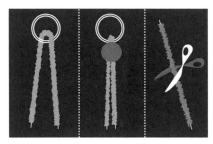

4 Cut the second pipe cleaner in half.

5 Place half of the cut pipe-cleaner just under the head; fold the left side over to the right, and the right side over to the left to create the arms.

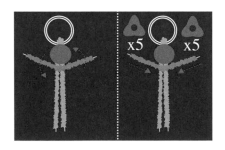

6 Thread five of the triangular beads on each arm.

7 Now gather two snowflake beads and put one on each arm, securing them against the other beads. Wrap the pipe cleaner around every other point of the snowflake bead to secure it. Cut off the extra length of piper cleaner, and make sure to tuck in the sharp metal parts.

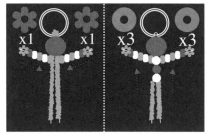

8 Push three of the pony beads onto the body, over both ends of the pipe cleaner, and pull them up as far as they will go. They should come up against the middle of the arms to form the torso.

9 Spread the ends of the bottom pipe cleaners to form

the legs. Place seven triangular beads on each leg, again pushing up each one as high as it will go.

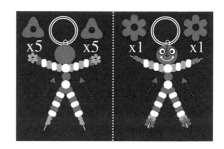

10 Push one snowflake bead onto each leg, coming up against the other beads, and wrap the pipe cleaner around every other point to secure it. Again, cut off the excess and make sure to hide any pointy ends of the pipe cleaner.

11 Decorate the face with paint or stickers, or add yarn with glue to the head to create hair.

Fuse Bead Fun

*O*nce your grandchildren are safely past the stage of putting every small object in their mouths and have developed reasonably good hand-eye coordination (around age 5) be sure to invest in a supply of fuse beads to have on hand at all times. These are tiny, colorful beads the children painstakingly place on specially designed pegboards in a variety of whimsical shapes, from animals and flowers to moons and stars. After the designs are complete, the supervising adult (that is, you) irons over the beads, fusing them together to form a permanent toy treasure. Fuse-bead projects can take hours to complete, making them the perfect diversion for a rainy day.

What you will need:

* ★ Fuse beads (also called activity beads or Perler beads; sold in large jugs or as part of a kit)
* ★ Pegboards (purchased separately or as part of a kit)
* ★ Parchment paper (one or two pieces cut into squares big enough to cover the design)
* ★ Iron

1 Set up the kids at an empty table with plenty of flat surface space. They will need lots of elbow room.

2 Pour beads into individual bowls so the kids can easily get at them without jostling each others' boards.

3 Let them take their time completely filling their boards. The entire board must be covered so that each bead can be fused to its neighbor.

4 Carefully transfer the completed pegboard to a stable, heat-resistant surface for ironing. Granite countertops work well for this purpose if you have one, but an ironing board will also suffice. (Just make sure the ironing board is very stable.)

5 Heat the iron to a medium to high setting. Be sure the children understand that they are not to come near the ironing area anytime the iron is hot.

6 Place the parchment paper carefully over the beads and pegboard and begin to iron slowly. The initial touch with the iron must be smooth and firm: The beads will immediately begin to fuse, so if you pull up too early, you risk pulling up the beads. Slowly run the iron over the entire surface of the

paper covering the design. After about three to five minutes, lift the paper slowly and check the progress. The beads should have melted together, and most holes will close.

7 Let the piece cool briefly, and then carefully lift the fused design off the pegboard.

8 Turn the piece over and place it directly on the ironing surface. Place the parchment paper on top of the beads and iron as you did the first side.

9 Let the piece cool completely before handing it to your grandchild

Easy-as-Pie Apple Crumb Pie

*Y*ou might find the idea of baking an apple pie from scratch a bit daunting. The reason? For most of us, it's that from-scratch pie crust. The good news is that even if you are unaccustomed to working magic with a rolling pin, you and your grandkids can still make a fantastic homemade pie using any of a number of crust shortcuts, from premade crust shells to prerolled dough. You will still be able to top your creation with ice cream and serve it to the family with a straight face when you tell them you were careful not to overwork the dough. This recipe is a good combination of easy but not deceitful home baking that your grandkids are sure to enjoy making and eating.

What you will need for the pie:

- ★ 9-inch frozen pie crust in the tin
- ★ 1 cup sugar
- ★ 2 tsp. flour
- ★ ¼ tsp. nutmeg
- ★ ½ tsp. cinnamon
- ★ 6 cups peeled and thinly sliced tart apples
- ★ Crumb topping (recipe follows)

1 Preheat oven to 425°F.

2 Poke fork holes in bottom of slightly thawed pie crust. Bake for five minutes.

3 In a large bowl, mix sugar, flour, nutmeg, and cinnamon, using a large spoon.

4 Add the sliced apples to the sugar mixture.

5 Carefully pile apples into pie crust.

6 Top with crumb topping (see recipe, below).

What you will need for crumb topping:

- ★ ½ cup firmly packed light brown sugar
- ★ ¼ cup slightly softened butter cut into pieces
- ★ ⅓ cup sifted all-purpose flour
- ★ ¼ tsp. cinnamon

---

1 Blend ingredients with a fork until butter is the size of peas (perfect for little hands to do slowly).

2 With your hands, place and pat the crumb topping onto the apples to cover them completely.

3 Place the pie on a cookie sheet to catch any drippings.

4 Bake for 40 minutes or until the apples are tender and the crumb topping has turned golden brown.

Grandparents' Note

Be sure to read *How to Make an Apple Pie and See the World*, by Marjorie Priceman, to your grandchildren. This lovely picture book tells the story of a young girl who travels all over the world to gather ingredients to make her pie.

Top 10 Greatest Snacks
of All Time

*P*lain pretzels, Goldfish crackers, and corn chips are terrific quick snacks to have around for those moments when your grandkids just can't wait for a meal. But here are 10 suggestions for inventive snacks to offer when you feel like doing something a bit more unexpected.

Number 1
English Muffin or Bagel Pizza

What you will need:

★ English muffins or bagels (one half per child)

★ Pizza sauce (one to two tbsp. per half muffin or bagel)

★ Grated mozzarella cheese (about two tbsp. per half muffin or bagel)

1 Lightly toast the muffins or bagels in a toaster oven.

2 Remove from toaster and place on a small tray.

3 Spread sauce and sprinkle cheese on muffins or bagels.

4 Return to toaster oven and bake at about 325°F for 8 to 10 minutes or until cheese melts and starts to bubble.

Number 2
Fruit Skewers

What you will need:

★ Wooden skewers
  (2 per child)

★ Melon, apples, pears,
  grapes, and berries
  (about 6 pieces total
  per skewer)

Grandparents' Note

Instead of fruit, substitute
vegetables—cut-up cucumbers, cherry tomatoes, olives,
even a leaf of romaine
lettuce—and you've got
Greek salad on a stick!

1 Wash and cut the fruit into
  bite-sized portions.

2 Push the pieces of fruit
  onto the wooden skewers,
leaving the bottom inch fruit-
free so that little hands can
easily grasp them.

Number 3
Cone Sandwiches

What you will need:

★ Wafer ice-cream
  cone with flat bottom
  (1 per child)

★ Chicken, egg, or tuna
  salad (about one large ice-
  cream scoop per cone)

1 Simply scoop the salad into the top of the cone. Add more if desired. This snack can also serve as a fun lunch treat.

Number 4
Cake Cones

What you will need:

★ 1 box cake mix
★ 24 wafer ice-cream cones with flat bottoms
★ 2 12-muffin tins
★ 1 can icing
★ Sprinkles

1 Preheat oven and prepare the cake batter according to the cupcake directions on the box.

2 Stand the cones in the muffin tins, one in each cup, then carefully fill the cones with the prepared batter.

3 Carefully slide the muffin pans into the oven (be sure each pan will clear the oven racks), and bake according to directions on box. Use a toothpick to make sure the cake is cooked through.

4 Let cool.

5 Once the cones have cooled completely, decorate them with icing and sprinkles so they look like ice-cream cones.

Number 5
Chocolate-Covered Pretzels

What you will need:

* ★ One 12-ounce bag semi-sweet chocolate chips
* ★ Pretzels or pretzel rods (2 or 3 per child)
* ★ Sprinkles

1 In a microwave oven set at half power, melt the chocolate chips in a micro-wave-safe bowl. Or place the chocolate in a double boiler on the stovetop, carefully stirring to ensure a smooth consistency.

2 Pour the melted chocolate into a cool bowl so that it's safe for the children to handle.

3 Pour the sprinkles into a second shallow bowl.

4 Line a cookie sheet or similar-sized tray with wax or parchment paper.

5 Let the children take turns dipping half of the pretzel in the melted chocolate and then dipping it into the sprinkles bowl.

6 Place the pretzels on the lined tray. Allow to cool and enjoy!

Grandparents' Note

Once you and your grandchildren master the art of chocolate dipping, dip cookies, crackers, raisins, bananas, frozen peanut butter—pretty much anything that tastes good with chocolate.

Number 6
Ladybugs on a Log

What you will need:

★ 1 bunch washed celery
★ 1 8-ounce box cream cheese
★ 8 ounces dried cranberries

1 Separate the celery stalks and slice into three- to four-inch-long pieces, discarding any extra. Each stalk should yield about two logs.

2 Using a butter knife, spread the celery stalk grooves with cream cheese.

3 Sprinkle dried cranberries over the cream cheese. Enjoy this colorful and crunchy snack!

Grandparents' Note

For a different taste, substitute the cream cheese with peanut butter and the dried cranberries with raisins, dried cherries, dried blueberries, and the like.

Number 7
Shape Sandwiches

What you will need:

★ Soft bread

▲ Peanut butter, jelly, honey, cream cheese— pretty much any sandwich spread

★ Cookie cutters

1 Shape sandwiches are basically sandwiches with one special twist: Once you make the individual sandwiches using your grandkids' favorite ingredients, let them cut out shapes using a variety of cookie cutters. Save the remaining crusts and bread-only remnants for feeding your backyard birds.

Number 8
Tropical Smoothies

What you will need:

▲ Fresh or frozen berries (handful per smoothie)

★ Banana (optional)

★ Plain or vanilla yogurt (one 8-ounce container per smoothie)

★ Ice cubes

★ Milk or fruit juice as needed to thin the consistency

1 Put all the ingredients in a blender. Your grandchildren can help with this part, but make sure their fingers are well out of the way of the blades.

2 Secure the lid and mix the ingredients.

3 Serve in a cup with a festive straw and fancy umbrella.

Number 9
Orange Frozen Smoothie Pops

What you will need:

★ 1 can frozen concentrated orange juice

★ 1 12-ounce package soft tofu

★ 2 cups unflavored soy milk

★ Plastic or silicone pop mold tray (with room for 8 to 12 pops) and sticks

1 Combine all ingredients in a blender or using a hand mixer.

2 Pour mixture into pop mold tray, insert sticks, and freeze until solid (4 to 5 hours).

3 Drink up any of the leftover mix for a cool and tasty treat on the spot!

What you will need:

★ Vanilla, chocolate, or strawberry ice cream (really, any flavor will do)

★ Chocolate, hot fudge, caramel, butterscotch, strawberry, or marshmallow sauce

★ Chocolate chips, peanut butter chips, mini marshmallows, M&M candies, crushed pretzels, peanuts, crushed cookies, whipped cream, cherries

1 Gather the grandkids and take a trip to the store to forage for ingredients. The only rule is that the toppings you choose must taste good on ice cream.

2 Once home, dish the ice cream into bowls. Put all the toppings out on the table in individual serving bowls with spoons and let everyone serve themselves.

3 Have the children pour on the syrup topping first, then a dry topping, and finish with the whipped cream and cherry on top. They can do it any way they want as long as it tastes good!

Grandparents' Note

For an added touch, make this activity into a taste challenge, with you as the judge. The best-tasting sundae is awarded a special gold ribbon.

Make a Good-Times Diorama

*I*s there one particular beach you always go to with your grandchildren—the one you think longingly about over the winter? Or a holiday dinner you repeat each year that your grandkids would like to remember on the other 364 days of the year? Or an afternoon at the park you all would like to relive every once in a while? Make a diorama that captures those moments: a miniature tableau depicting the wonderful time you and your grandchildren shared.

What you will need:

★ 1 shoebox or other box that can be stood on one side (the base should measure at least 14 inches)

★ Prop materials (see #3)

★ Glue or a hot glue gun

★ Washable paint (one set with 5 primary colors)

1 Decide on a scene for the diorama. If no vacations, holidays, or shared afternoons come to mind but your grandchildren have particular interests, like animals or dinosaurs, build the scene around them. Or consider creating a scene from a book you enjoyed reading together.

2 Have the children list or sketch all the items the diorama will contain, including the floor, the furniture, the people, and all the special details that depict the scene.

3 Take a trip together to the crafts store and purchase some miniature items for a dollhouse, or make the props from scratch: Fashion a table from the plastic insert that pizza restaurants use to prevent cheese from touching the top of the box; cut out scraps of fabric for curtains or a tablecloth; gather sand from the beach to use as the foundation for a beach scene. Brainstorm with your grandchildren. With this activity, finding and making the miniature items will be half the fun.

4 Decide which way the box will be oriented. Typically, it should stand on its wider side so that the scene is displayed on the inside bottom and back of the box. Just make sure it can sit stably on a flat surface.

5 Paint the box interior. Choose a color that coordinates with the scene: bright blue for the summer sky, green for the forest surrounding a campsite, and so forth. The children can choose to paint the outside too, depending on whether there are any designs or logos to cover.

6 Let the paint dry completely. While you wait, have the children paint and add details to the miniature furniture and other props.

7 Help the children construct the floor: Grass can be depicted with small pieces of green yarn; a beach with sand; a rug with felt or carpet scraps; and a wooden floor with Popsicle sticks. Let them glue the material to the inside bottom of the box.

8 Encourage the children to build the rest of the scene, securing the bigger, foundation pieces first (furniture, trees, etc.). Then let them fill in the smaller items and detailing. Should there be a painting on the wall? If so, they can draw or paint one on a small piece of paper and glue it to the inside

back of the box. Maybe you have shells left over from your beach trip: Have the kids glue them onto the sand foundation. If the diorama depicts a holiday meal, have your grandchildren draw or construct food platters, napkins, silverware, and so forth from paper or cardboard.

9 Once the scene is complete, let everything dry. Take the time to discuss where you'll display the diorama. Perhaps it will become a permanent fixture in the room where the kids usually sleep during overnights at your home.

Create a Family Fun Box

*n*o doubt your grandchildren already eagerly anticipate their visits to your home, but there's no better way to welcome them back than with a box of fun created especially for them. A fun box is a dedicated cardboard or plastic container filled with crayons, markers, small toys, stickers, paints, and even comic books, depending on the child's age and specific tastes and interests. Keep the box in the same place so they can easily reach it. It will be a small part of your home they can always call their own.

1 You can either buy a large, lidded plastic storage box from an office-supply store or simply recycle a sturdy cardboard box you already have on hand. Boxes measuring about two square feet are ideal: They'll contain plenty of materials and be easy to store.

2 Paint or decorate the box as you wish, using markers, cut-out letters, or paints. You might choose to emblazon the box with "Jacob's Fun Box" or "Julie's Box of Tricks." Get creative, and use their favorite colors to depict the activities, themes, and animals they love best. Feel free to attach glitter, stickers, and photos for a truly festive look.

3 Now give some thought to the items you know will keep your grandchildren occupied: crayons, coloring books, stickers and sticker books, find-the-hidden-picture books, small plastic animals, picture books, Play-Doh, and miniature cars or trucks. Depending on the child's particular interests, you can include plastic army men, mini fairy or princess figures, small dolls, small Lego kits, and glitter pens. Markers, crayons, and blank books are

always appealing for boys and girls alike.

4 As you go about your everyday activities and errands, keep the boxes in mind. If you come across a potential fun box item—a great pine cone you find in your yard, a cool mini prism you see in a shop window—place it in the box for your grandchild's next visit. She'll love pulling off that box top to discover the new (and old) treasures inside!

Build a Gingerbread House

*E*veryone dreams of making the perfect gingerbread house from scratch, but most people never dream they can actually do it. All that baking and cooling and cutting and building is a bit daunting, even for the craftiest of grandparents. Here is an incredibly easy recipe for a gingerbread house anyone can create. Make it with your grandchildren when they come for a holiday visit or as a way to use up some of that leftover Halloween or Easter candy.

What you will need:

★ 1 paper plate

★ Pastry or plastic bag with hole cut in one tip (optional—you can use a plastic knife or fingers instead)

★ Graham crackers

★ 1 12-ounce can vanilla frosting

★ 5 12-ounce bags of assorted candies (gumdrops, gummy bears, M&Ms, chocolate chips, etc.)

1 Put a layer of frosting on the bottom of the plate. Just use enough so that the graham cracker pieces will stand up.

2 Dab frosting onto the sides of 4 graham crackers and arrange the pieces in a box on the plate. Note that frosting serves as the "glue" throughout this project. (You may want to

use a small box or milk carton as a base onto which you "glue" the crackers.)

3 Cut a cracker into two triangular pieces; these will form the peak of the house. Then attach two more pieces to the top to form the roof.

4 Now, again using the frosting as glue, let the children decorate the house with the candy however they like. They'll simply dab a little frosting on the back of the candy pieces and stick them to the house. Help them make windows or the outline of a door. They can also make a path on the plate leading away from the house. If they want to use colors other than white for detailing, let

them add a little food coloring to the frosting.

5 Allow the frosting to dry completely overnight.

6 Have the children decide where best to display their gingerbread house for the greatest visual impact: in the window, on a mantel, or as a holiday centerpiece.

Fun-with-Paper Projects

*P*aper is an abundant, multipurpose, and relatively inexpensive supply to have around the house for any number of kids' games and crafts. If you're all stuck indoors on a rainy or snowy day, try some of these crafty projects.

Paper Chains

What you will need:

★ Plenty of multicolored 8½ x 11–inch construction paper (alternatively, have the kids use markers and paints to add designs to basic white paper)

★ Child-friendly safety scissors

★ Stapler loaded with staples (use glue sticks if the kids are too young to handle a stapler)

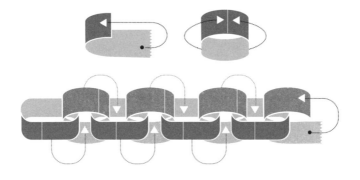

1 Show the children how to cut the paper into strips that are about 8 inches long and about 2 inches wide. (If the children are going to color or decorate the paper strips, have them do so now. Let the decorated strips dry.)

2 Have the children fold the first strip into a circle, bringing one end up to meet the other and then either stapling or gluing the overlapping ends together.

3 Let the children take another strip and loop it through the first circle, making another circle that is intertwined with the first. Staple or glue the end closed.

4 The children will repeat this process until they have a long chain. They can use the chains for garlands to decorate a Christmas tree, succah, or even the guest room where they may be sleeping during their stay.

Construction-Paper Sailor Hat

What you will need:

* ★ 1 sheet of 20 x 16–inch construction paper (if you can't find the right size, get something larger and cut it down)
* ★ Child-friendly safety scissors
* ★ Tape
* ★ Pencil

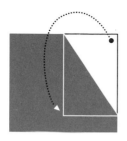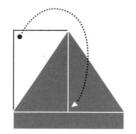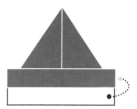

1 Have the child fold the construction paper in half so that one short end meets the other.

2 With the folded seam at the top, fold the top left corner over to the center, leaving about an inch or two of paper clearance at the bottom.

3 Let him fold the top right corner over to the center to meet the top left corner.

4 Have him fold up the strip of paper below the folded corners, then flip the hat over to the opposite side to fold up the other bottom strip.

5 Open the end, place on head, and it's off to sea!

Paper Airplane

What you will need:

★ 1 sheet colored or white 8½ x 11–inch paper

1 Have the child fold the paper in half, long end to long end.

2 Unfold, and using the center crease as a guide, fold

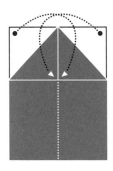
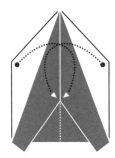

the top left and right corners in halfway so that each corner touches the center line.

3 Fold each corner again on top of the first fold so that they meet at the center.

4 Fold in half at the first crease again so that the

front of the paper now forms a point.

5 With the tip pointing away from you in a ready-to-fly position, fold each wing at the back of the plane down toward the ground. Take to the air!

Paper Flowers

What you will need:

★ Many sheets of colorful tissue paper (a dozen sheets per flower)

★ Pipe cleaners (1 green

pipe cleaner per stem, but any color will do in a pinch)

★ Child-friendly safety scissors

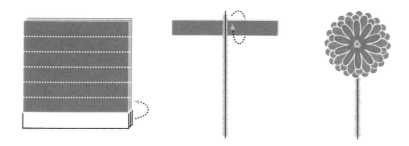

1 Have the child layer 10 or 12 (or more) pieces of tissue paper, using either one color or several different colors, depending on her preference. Have her cut the bunch into a square about 8 inches by 8 inches (this can vary according to the desired size of the flower).

2 Keeping the layers intact, she'll fold the square like an accordion: first folding the edge over itself, then flipping the piece over to fold it back over again, until the entire square is folded into a thin strip about an inch wide or slightly thinner.

3 Have her wind one end of the piper cleaner around the center of the paper strip, with the remaining length brought down to form the stem. She can add another pipe cleaner to the first by twisting one onto the other for a longer stem.

4 Have her gently spread out the layers of paper on both sides so that each layer forms its own petal.

5 At this point, she can fluff up the petals to conceal the wire stem.

6 She can make an entire bouquet if she likes! The flowers make a great gift or a bright table centerpiece when placed in a vase.

Afternoon Tea and Scone Treats

*A*fternoon tea is traditionally served in the late afternoon, around 4 P.M. It has the reputation as a fussy event where dainty ladies drink hot beverages with their pinkies sticking out, but there's no reason you can't create your own version for the grandkids. Have them invite a few dolls, teddy bears, princesses, or favorite superheroes. Or they can invite friends and neighbors or other family members. If you think your grandchildren can handle it, use your best china. If not, any plates and mugs will do.

Delicious Home-Baked Scones

This scone recipe comes courtesy of a café in Ocean City, New Jersey, called Who's On 1st, formerly the Fourth Street Café. These scones are so good that people plan their summer vacations around which flavors are available on specific days! The amazing thing is, they can be just as good when made at home—as long as you don't overmix them.

What you will need:

* ★ 6 cups flour
* ★ ½ tsp. salt
* ★ 1 tsp. baking soda
* ★ 2 tbs. plus 2 tsp. baking powder
* ★ 1 cup sugar (plus a little extra for sprinkling)
* ★ 2 sticks softened butter
* ★ 2 cups buttermilk
* ★ ½ pound chips or berries (anything from blueberries and raspberries to butterscotch or chocolate chips)
* ★ Egg wash (½ cup milk mixed with 1 egg)

Makes 16–20 scones

1 Preheat the oven to 400°F. Grease and flour a flat cookie sheet or jelly-roll pan.

2 Mix together flour, salt, baking soda, baking powder, and sugar. This is a great task for your grandchild since it doesn't involve handling anything hot. Measure each dry ingredient and mix them all together.

3 Have your grandchild cut in butter using butter knives or a scraper's edge. The butter should be added slowly, taking care not to overmix.

4 Add buttermilk and chips or berries. Again, be careful not to overmix the batter. It should look as if it is almost falling apart.

5 Turn the dough out onto a lightly floured surface and direct your grandchild to gently roll or push dough into a square about 1½ half inches thick. Use a biscuit cutter to cut the dough into shapes. Alternatively, use a knife to cut the dough into the traditional triangles. Just be sure not to handle it too much.

6 Gently transfer the scones onto the greased and floured pan.

7 Brush egg wash over the scones and sprinkle with sugar.

8 Bake for 10 minutes at 400°F and then reduce the temperature to 300°F and bake an additional 20 minutes.

Setting Up the Tea Party

1 While the scones are baking, have the children choose the tea. They might like a decaffeinated tea flavored with peppermint or apple cinnamon. Let your grandchildren drop the teabags into the pot.

2 Help the children set the table. For a fancy setting, use cloth napkins. The children can cut doilies out of paper to decorate the table or place on plates below the scones.

3 If the children wish, you can all get dressed up in your party clothes, or maybe even wear fancy hats or superhero capes.

4 When the scones are ready, put them on the table along with the teapot and pour in some boiling water to allow the tea to steep. (Allow to cool before sipping!) If they would prefer hot chocolate or simple hot milk, you can comply with their wishes—it's their party, after all!

5 Relax and enjoy each other's company. If there is a lull in the conversation, you can read aloud from Lewis Carroll's *Alice in Wonderland*. The chapter about the mad tea party would be particularly appropriate.

Grandparent Wisdom

WHAT ARE THE BEST OR WORST GIFTS YOU HAVE GIVEN TO YOUR GRANDCHILDREN?

" Sending my youngest grandson to a water camp for sailing. He loves it!"

Lois, grandmother of 6

" To show them love and affection, caring and understanding, and teach them values. "

—Victor, grandfather of 3

" Best gifts: books, U.S. quarters [from each of the] states, and a map of the U.S. with slots for quarters. Setting up an investment fund. Worst gifts: The messy ones—but they were great fun! "

—Bonnie, grandmother of 3

" Best gift: an iPod. My granddaughter listens to books on it while she's quilting or beading in bed. "

—Judy, grandmother of 1

" My artistic ability, some of my temper, and the gumption to just go ahead and do something new. "

—Mary Ellen, grandmother of 3

" Best gifts: dress-up play clothes, Legos, canvas, jars of paint, and paintbrushes. "

—Nancy, grandmother of 5

Sharing and Exploring the World Together

*I*t might be every grandparent's dream to take their grandchildren on a trip to an exotic locale to explore a new place together. And perhaps that's something you will do someday. But as you'll find in the pages that follow, there is so much to explore close to home that you won't even need to board a plane.

You can indulge your travel bug by investigating the ethnic restaurants in your town and choosing one for a special meal with the grandkids. The cuisine might seem foreign to little mouths, but it's a whole lot easier than packing your bags and booking a hotel. You and your grandchildren can visit the past, present, and future simply by playing a time-machine game in the comfort of your living room, or get to know the landscape around you by taking a ride on the local train line and making an afternoon of it. Expand your own universe by taking a trip to your grandchild's school to find out how he spends his day, whom he plays with, and what he's learning. Discover the natural world where you and your grandchild live by taking walks in the woods or just around the block.

Discovery and *adventure* are two words you will always want to remember when it comes to spending precious time with your grandchildren. There's no better way to relive the excitement and wonder of new experiences than with a little one at your side, for whom every adventure with Grandma or Grandpa is a thrill!

Make Trail Mix and Hit the Trails!

*K*ids love to mix things together. They also love having a plan and a goal. On a beautiful day when you don't have any other activities planned, gather your grandkids for a trail mix and hiking adventure.

1 Begin by making a list of trail mix ingredients, letting your grandchildren help with the choices. You can talk about mixing sweet with salty, crunchy with chewy, and explain how some of the items will give them a quick burst of energy, but others will give them energy for the long haul and let them walk farther. Choose at least one ingredient from each of the following categories (or use them all):

Dried fruit: cranberries, blueberries, pineapple, banana chips, apples, raisins
Nuts (omit if any of the children have nut allergies): peanuts, cashews, almonds, hazelnuts, walnuts, pecans
Salty snacks: pretzel sticks, mini pretzels, goldfish crackers
Sweet snacks: chocolate chips, mini marshmallows, peanut butter chips (omit if allergies are an issue), butterscotch chips, M&M candies
Crispy snacks: dry cereals or granola

2 Take a shopping excursion together to procure your provisions.

3 Once you have your ingredients, invite your grandchildren to help you measure out equal parts of all the ingredients into a large bowl, use a big spoon to stir it all together, and then portion out the mix into plastic storage bags.

4 Seal the bags closed and instruct the children to dance around the room and shake their bags so that the ingredients mix together.

5 With individual bags of trail mix and small bottles of water in hand, you can all set out for a hiking adventure. Is there a nature center near you? A hiking trail? Don't be too ambitious: Know what you can handle, but also what your grandchildren can handle. You can always hike out to the nearest park bench or even out to the backyard to enjoy the tasty trail treats.

Setting Goals

If hiking turns out to be an activity your grandchildren enjoy, plan on regular excursions.

1 Begin slowly and build up: Set short distance goals at first (one or two blocks, 5 minutes of hiking, etc.) and then increase the hike as the children begin to gain stamina and confidence. You don't want to be a mile into a walk and have one of your grandchildren refuse to go on.

2 Be sure to tell the children how much distance you will cover in your hike, and give them landmarks to gauge how far they've traveled and how far they still have to go. This will let them feel in control of the hike and decrease the chances of a midhike meltdown.

Top 10 Tips for a Day at the Museum or Zoo

*W*hen you and the kids grow tired of hanging around the house all day and want to do something fun, a day at a local museum, zoo, aquarium, or another attraction is a great idea. But you need to be prepared. Here are 10 tips to keep in mind while planning your day.

1. Bring a stroller. Even if your grandchild uses it only on occasion and insists he's too old for it, bring it along (you can always use it to cart your bags and other gear). After hours of watching gorillas and giraffes or sharks and fish, he will be grateful for the chance to sit down. Just make sure the venue allows strollers in the exhibits.

2. Go early in the day—before naps or lunch if possible. Avoid a grumpy child's meltdown by getting to your destination well before pre-nap crankiness and hunger take hold.

3. Know exactly where and when you are going to eat. Is there a café just beyond the bear exhibit? Or a restaurant at the museum? Or a great little diner down the street from the aquarium? Whatever it is, have it set and agreed upon before you head out. The last thing you want is an irritable, hungry kid waiting in a long line you didn't anticipate.

4. Bring along small snacks and water if possible. You don't want to weigh yourself down, but a small bag of pretzels or graham crackers and a couple bottles of water will go a long way toward satisfying the child's hunger until you get to lunch.

5. Keep your eye out for bathrooms and never miss an opportunity to go. Survey the venue's map before you get too engrossed in an exhibit so that you have an idea of where the closest bathrooms are when someone has to go fast. Whenever you pass a bathroom, encourage your grandchild to use it.

6. Always put safety first and supervise your grandchild at all times. So long as he or she is still small, you may take your opposite-sex grandchildren into the restroom with you. If you feel this is inappropriate, or that other visitors might be offended, stand within earshot while your grandchild uses the bathroom. After the child reaches the age of 12, use your own discretion to determine if he or she can head in there alone.

7. **Determine whether the day is a "no-gift day" or a "gift day" before you enter.** Many exhibits dump you right into the gift shop, often ending the fun in a tantrum after you say no to an expensive puzzle. If today is a gift day, set a limit on the price of the item. If it is a no-gift day, let the child know when she might next expect a little something (an upcoming birthday or holiday) to give her something to look forward to.

8. **As soon as you arrive, discuss what you'll see.** Let each child you're traveling with choose one destination, and let those stops be your main goals for the day.

9. **Stay together, but have a plan if someone gets lost.** Carefully point out the location of security guards and instruct the child to ask a guard (*not* a stranger) for help if she's lost. If the child is old enough to read and understand signage, set an agreed-upon meeting place. (If your grandchild gets out of your sight for a second, take a deep breath and look carefully in your immediate area. Chances are she is just behind the person blocking your view.)

10. **Leave while everyone is still having fun.** This will prevent meltdowns and tantrums and terrible walks to the car, and it will allow you all to look forward to your next outing.

Dining Out, Kid-Style: A Survival Guide

*T*aking young children to restaurants can be a challenge. Kids get antsy, often have limited food preferences, and, of course, possess an uncanny ability to pick up on their adult company's anxiety. But there's no need for you to resort to fast-food chains. Once your grandchildren are older than eight or so, outing out can be a treat. You might choose to take your grandchild to a more elegant restaurant than he or she has ever been to as a way to show off your hometown or explore the world through ethnic cuisine. Going to India with an eight-year-old might be tough, but trying steam-puffed poori breads at an Indian restaurant can introduce him to a whole new world of tastes and wonder about the world beyond his own. Here are a few tips for making dining out fun for everyone, regardless of your grandchild's age:

* Locate restaurants that welcome young children by asking whether they offer highchairs and booster seats. Some of even the most high-end restaurants will happily pull out a highchair when asked, so call around beforehand.
* Look for large-ish restaurants that offer an easy place to escape to—a hotel lobby or a bookstore—when the kids reach their limits before the meal is over.
* Don't forget sippy cups and bibs for your youngest grandchildren.
* If there is nothing obvious on the menu for your grandchildren to eat, ask the waitstaff if the chef can make something simple. Usually, if they bothered to bring out the highchair, they will be willing to make plain pasta or grilled chicken. Scan the menu and make some suggestions yourself if the choices are otherwise uninspiring.

✳ Always have a few tricks up your sleeve: Review some of the suggestions below. Just make sure not to bring along projects so large that there won't be room for food on the table!

A RESTAURANT SURVIVAL KIT

Take along the following for your next restaurant excursion with your grandchild:

✳ Coloring books, stickers, blank pieces of paper, and markers or crayons
✳ Mini Lego projects or mini puzzles
✳ A book to read to the child while waiting for food to arrive
✳ A deck of cards
✳ Lollipops—if all else fails

A Visit from the Tooth Fairy

*I*f your grandchild is scheduled to stay with you and arrives with a loose tooth, you'll want to (discreetly) discuss Tooth Fairy policy with the parents before he's left in your care. Does said Tooth Fairy have a name? Is there a backstory? Does the fairy leave money, a toy, a note? You want to be consistent, and you don't want to go overboard. (If you give the child $30 for a tooth, for example, how will the parents keep up after that?)

If the loose tooth doesn't make itself known until after the parents have departed, ask your grandchild what the Tooth Fairy typically brings. (If he is savvy enough to tell you that the Tooth Fairy brings him video games, for example, he's probably figured out the whole thing and you don't need to worry so much about keeping up the charade.)

Do not pull the tooth, no matter how much your grandchild begs. Let it take its own time. Here is what to do if that tooth just won't wait:

1 Immediately put the tooth in a baggie or envelope.

2 Together with your grandchild, place the tooth under the child's pillow just before bedtime, making sure to keep it as accessible as possible so you can easily retrieve it later.

3 Wait for the child to fall deeply asleep (and be sure not to fall asleep yourself!).

4 Once the child is asleep, retrieve the tooth and gently place your gift just slightly under the pillow. Hide the tooth in a safe place until you are able to discreetly give it to the parents.

As far as your fairy gift goes, follow the parents' lead:

- If they told you to keep it simple and push a few quarters under the pillow, then do so.
- If it is their tradition to write a note, take care to disguise your writing so that your grandchild can't recognize it (try writing it with your non-dominant hand if you are a bad faker). You can always tell him that the Tooth Fairy broke her finger trying to lift an extra-large tooth, and that's why the writing looks funny.
- If you want to do something very special (put in extra money or a small piece of jewelry), then leave a note saying you are a local Tooth Fairy who is filling in for the usual one. This will allow the parents to go back to their normal practice the next time the Tooth Fairy visits.

Cue the Fairy Dust!

Fairy dust from the Tooth Fairy is always a great surprise gift if you want to do something special but aren't sure just what.

What you will need:

- ★ Glitter (gold or silver works best)
- ★ Dried flowers (lavender, small leaves, etc.)
- ★ Small plastic bag
- ★ Piece of ribbon

1 Pour glitter into the bag, one-quarter to one-third full.

2 Crush the dried flowers or leaves into the glitter.

3 Tie the bag with the ribbon and place under the child's pillow. The next day, everyone can make a wish!

Top 4 Tricks for Staying in Touch with Your Grandchildren

*I*t's never easy to live far from the people you love, particularly the small ones who change and grow constantly. One day they're crawling, and by the time you see them again they can walk. Here are suggestions to help close the distance between you just a bit.

Number 1: Read to Each Other

Reading a favorite book to each other on the phone is an expensive option, and one that might offer too many distractions. Instead, consider making a "book on tape" for your grandchild. Your grand-child may also be able to listen to the tapes on short car trips. Whatever the case, it will provide a wonderful way to hear your voice regularly. Once your grandchild begins to read, she may want to make her own recording of a favorite book or chapter to send to you, or you can each alternate taping chapters of one book.

1 Check out a book from the library your grandchild knows and loves or one you knew and loved as a child.

2 Using a dependable tape recorder, record yourself reading the book. (Check with the parents to make sure they have the equipment to play the tapes.)

3 Label the cassette and mail if off to your grand-child in an extra-special mailer addressed to him or her.

Number 2: Imagine Map Routes

1 On your grandchild's next visit, give him a map that shows all the routes between your homes.

2 Draw different routes and imagine the landmarks you would see along the way: Would you pass the Grand Canyon? Crater Lake? the Statue of Liberty? If you dipped slightly to the south, would you hit the Great Smokey Mountains? the Alamo?

3 Mark the landmarks on the map with stickers, and be sure your grandchild takes the map home. This is a great opportunity for you both to get to know the country together, and it's a way for your grandchild to think about you while you are apart.

4 The next time you speak to him, be sure to ask about the landmarks and other sites he saw on the way home.

Number 3: Start a Blog

A family blog is a quick and easy way to stay in touch and up-to-date on all the family news. Simply go to the Web site www.blogspot.com, which will take you through the steps for setup. If your grandchild is old enough to read, write, and use a computer on her own, she can access the page whenever she wants (parents allowing, of course), and add her photos, thoughts, and goings-on. If your grandchild is still tiny, her parents can write and update the blog.

Number 4: Share World News

Before your grandchild is old enough to read a newspaper, you and his parents will no doubt be hiding horrific front page pictures and hoping the child doesn't understand the headlines. But once he starts reading on his own and accessing the Internet and other media, there is no going back.

Find an interesting event or topic that you both can follow through your local newspapers: an upcoming national election, the environment, a drought that is causing a food shortage somewhere in the world. Make sure you choose something that is big enough news to make it into *both* of your hometown papers. A topic might not be reported on every day, but searching for it will motivate the child to read through the newspaper, and even the fact that there's no news will give you something to share and discuss.

On a weekly basis, check in with each other by phone or e-mail to share what you've read.

Travel Through Time Together

*O*ne of the most amazing things about grandparenting is that you and your grandkids' lives span so many years. From the time you were a child till the day your first grandchild was born, the world witnessed enormous changes in technology, politics, and other social transformations. The things your grandchildren take for granted—televisions, computers, video games—were not the same things you took for granted, and so teaching this new generation about the past will uncover untold moments of wonder.

Here's a very simple game to play that will open up windows not just on the past but also on the present—allowing the kids to teach you a thing or two about the world as they know it.

The Past, Present, and Future Game

Your "time machine" will be a simple spinner that you can construct yourselves.

What you will need:

- ★ 8½-by-11-inch sheet of soft cardboard
- ★ 8½-by-11-inch sheet of white paper
- ★ Glue
- ★ Paper fastener (the type with a flat circle and two arms that secure on the back)

1 Cut a 6- or 7-inch circle out of the white paper and glue it to the center of the cardboard.

2 Using the markers, divide the circle into pie wedges with three even slices labeled PAST, PRESENT, and FUTURE. The children can decorate the surrounding board and the spinner face as much as they wish.

3 Use a scrap of the white paper to cut out an arrow. Leave the end opposite the arrow point large enough to support the paper fastener. Let the children color the arrow so that it will stand out.

4 Push the points of the paper fastener through the arrow, the spinner face, and the cardboard, then secure it to the back of the board. The spinner should remain loose enough so that it can easily be flicked to the "Past," "Present," and "Future" pie wedges.

Now it's time to play:

1 Seat everyone in a circle on the floor and start the game in motion by setting the arrow to "Past."

2 Dim the lights and have all players close their eyes while you describe what life was like when you were their age. Describe the foods you ate, the school you attended, what you did for fun, places you traveled to, and what sorts of cars your parents drove. Was there a color TV? Was there a TV at all? Did you have a shared phone line (known as a party line) or a phone just for your family? Did a milkman deliver milk to your door? What was happening in the country at the time? Who was the president? What was going on in the world? What was your first memory of a historic event, and how did you learn of it? Be sure to let the kids ask their own questions, as these subjects are sure to spark their curiosity.

3 Now let the child to your right take his turn. He can either spin the arrow or set it to a time period of his choosing. For example, he might choose to set the arrow to "Present" to talk about all of the things that occupy his time today, from computers to texting to DVDs.

4 Let each child take a turn, choosing a period to describe in detail. The "Future" category can provide everyone with the opportunity to imagine and talk about what life might be like in the next 50 years, when they become grandparents themselves!

Take a Ride on a Train or Bus

Cars, trucks, buses, planes, and trains are objects of fascination for many young children, and your grandchildren are probably not exceptions. They may have had plenty of car rides in their early years, but trying out other forms of transportation will give them a real thrill. Plan a day around taking a ride on a train or bus or any other sort of vehicle they've never ridden before. You may think of a bus or subway ride as the most mundane experience in the world, but once you look at it through the eyes of your grandchild, you'll remember why they hold so much fascination.

Not all towns have trains, but most have buses. If you're lucky enough to have both, you might decide to take the bus in the morning and head back on the train. Make the choice based on your grandchild's preference. Remember that it's not the destination but the journey that's most important. Plan to take the train or bus to another town, playground, or library—or even just to the train or bus station; have lunch; and then head home.

Get a map that shows the route you will be traveling. Bring along snacks and drinks, and make sure to take your grandchild to the bathroom before you set out.

Let your grandchild pay the fare. He'll take great pleasure in handing the money or token to the bus driver or conductor, and extra tokens or ticket stubs will make for wonderful souvenirs of this special trip.

Enjoy the ride. Try to sit near the front if possible, and see if you can't get the bus driver or train conductor to talk to your grandchild about the special buttons and dials that operate the vehicle. Let your grandchild be the one to ring the "stop" bell on the bus or listen for the announcement of your station stop.

Yellow Light Activities:
When to Proceed with Caution

*I*t is possible—likely even—that you will be able to make it to the top of the lighthouse your grandkids have always wanted to visit, despite that your knees have been bothering you lately and you have been slightly more out of breath than usual. But when it comes to engaging in physical activities with your grandkids, you need to take care that you don't push yourself beyond what's comfortable. The last thing you want to do is lead the kids on an exciting adventure and then have to turn back because you've made it as far as you can go. The following "Yellow Light Activities" are a reminder to slow down and proceed with caution when planning your next adventure.

Lighthouses: Most lighthouses call for significant climbing to the top and the lookout deck. Make sure you know how high and how steep the climb will be—not only for you but also for the littlest children in your group.

Paddle and row boats: You'll likely be doing all the rowing if your grandkids are not old enough to pitch in, so be sure to consider the currents and how far you plan to go. Rowing can get tiring, and you don't want to find yourself in the middle of a lake without the energy to get back. Similarly, while paddle boats at a zoo or amusement park may look like smooth sailing, they also require a lot of leg exertion (if your grandchildren have short legs, you'll be doing all the paddling, of course). Ask the attendant how far you have to go and whether you can take a shortcut back if the trip proves more tiring than you expect.

Zoo trips: Zoos can mean hours of walking, and, depending on the layout of the facility, you may have to walk the entire way through the park to get back to the exit. Before you go, find out how far the path around the zoo is and whether there are ways to get back more quickly if you need to.

Boardwalk surries: Surries allow you to peddle along boardwalks in a leisurely style. They may look effortless, but fill them with all your grandchildren and in no time they get heavy and hard to move forward, especially if you're doing all the peddling. Tell your grandchildren that you can all take a test ride for a block before you commit to a longer excursion. If the kids know the plan, they'll be less disappointed should you need to cut the ride short.

Apple and peach picking: Fruit picking may involve climbing trees and carrying heavy loads, not to mention sometimes having to hike to the orchards beforehand. If you're not in shape for this sort of adventure, find a farm that drives you to the trees and that has low-hanging fruit and/or sturdy ladders. Come prepared with a collapsible rolling cart to carry the fruit back with you.

Walking tours: City walks are less daunting than hiking into the wilderness because there are always cafes you can stop into and cabs you can take back if the walk is too long. All the same, be sure your grandchildren understand that you may need to resort to one of these options if the walking proves too tiring for any of you.

Visiting Your Grandchild's Classroom

A visit to your grandchild's school will give you a good sense of how he spends his time—and give him the chance to show you off to his teacher and friends. If you have more than one grandchild in the same school, offer to spend a set amount of time with each class. Consider these activities:

Read a book to the class. Many schools welcome guest readers as long as they have some advance notice. Talk to your grandchild about what he might like you to read, then choose a book that is age-appropriate for the class. Just remember to keep it short—kids get antsy quick.

Bake a special snack. Ask your grandchild's parents to set up a day when you can bring a snack to school. (Just make sure you know the school's policy regarding foods containing nuts and other possible allergens.) You can either decide with your grandchild what you will bring or make it a surprise. Perhaps there was a special treat you used to bring to school for your own kids; if so, you'll have a ready-made story to tell while everyone munches on the snack.

Contribute to the class theme or studies. Check with your grandchild to see what subjects they are tackling and determine whether you have some area of expertise to present to his class that would bring their studies to life. Perhaps it's your line of work, your country of origin, or a hobby that relates to the class's current coursework.

Offer to talk about a holiday or a family tradition. Maybe you always make a craft gift at Christmas and you would like to show the class how to make their own. Or you might consider bringing in apples and honey around Rosh Hashanah to show the tradition of ushering in a sweet new year.

Offer to chaperone a field trip. Talk about thrilling your grand children! Chaperoning a trip is the perfect way to help the school, get to know your grandchild's friends, and spend a special day together. Let your grandchild's parents know you would be interested in doing this so that they can arrange it with the school. This could also be a terrific gift to the parents, who might otherwise need to go on the trip themselves.

Tips for School Pickup Days

9f you live in the same town as your grandkids or are simply visiting, don't pass up the opportunity to volunteer for school pickup duty. This will give their parents a much-needed break (or a backup plan on very busy days), but it will also give you the chance to see your grandchildren in action with their peers and to get a full account about how they spent their day. There are a few things to keep in mind so that pickups go smoothly.

1 Make sure the parents notify the school that you will be doing pickup. Many schools will not discharge a student to a different family member without a formal request from the parents. In the case of a misunderstanding, be sure to have your cell phone with you, as well as the parents' cell phone numbers, so they can talk directly to the school staff.

2 Don't forget to transfer the car or booster seats to your car if the children are still young enough to need them. If you're unsure, ask the parents whether they're still required. (In the United States, state laws dictate that children must be of a certain age, height, and weight before they can forego the car seat/booster.)

3 Once you're at the school, ask your grandchildren if they want to give you a tour of the building or introduce you to their teachers. If the staff seems too busy for a visit, you can probably at least take a look at the children's classrooms and see their art on display.

4 Make sure your grandchildren have all the things they are supposed to bring home: lunch boxes, homework, notes from teachers, books to

read, and so forth. You don't want to have to return when they discover they forgot an important science project that's due tomorrow.

5 Now you get to use your grandparent's prerogative to take the kids for a special snack—something their parents might not normally do. Is there an ice cream shop nearby? Or a bakery? Take the time to have a little indulgence—so long as the children do not need to be home for naptime, of course.

6 If you are spending the afternoon with the children, offer to help them with their homework. This will give you the chance to see what they're learning these days and motivate them to get the work done. Their parents will be thrilled!

Plan a Special Meal Together

*I*f you have an entire day to spend with your grandchild, why not use it to plan and cook a special meal? Like many kids, he or she might not realize the steps that go into making a meal and will be fascinated to learn that it's not simply a matter of microwaving chicken nuggets.

1 Use the morning to browse through cookbooks in your kitchen or, better yet, at a favorite café where your grandchild can indulge in a special pastry treat. Talk about what types of food you each like. Discuss whom you might invite to this meal and how that might affect the menu choices. Decide if you want it to be a one-pot meal, such as a casserole, or a main dish and a few sides. Perhaps you can think back to your own favorite meal from when you were your grandchild's age and tell her everything you remember about the dish that made it your favorite.

2 Compile the guest list together and take turns making the phone calls to invite each guest (if the child is comfortable talking on the phone).

3 Next, have your grandchild write a list of every single ingredient you will need to prepare the meal. If she is too young to write, make the list together or let her draw pictures of the items.

4 Now it's off to the supermarket. Get your shopping cart and go up and down each aisle to find the ingredients you'll need. As you do so, share stories with your grandchild about how different food shopping was when you were young. Did your family go to a market like this? Did the milk and egg

deliveries come right to your house? Were there frozen pizzas and French fries back then?

5 After a few brief pointers, let your grandchild determine which tomatoes look good or which corn looks the sweetest or which meat looks the freshest. Take over only if you think something really doesn't look good.

6 Pick up something quick and easy for lunch on the way home. You both might be so focused on dinner that you won't realize how hungry you are. Use the mealtime to go over your menu and talk about the order in which you should prepare the meal. Write it down so that you and your grandchild can refer to the plan and get to work.

7 Consider your grandchild's age and give her the appropriate jobs. She might not be ready to boil the water, but she could fill the pot in the sink. She may not be old enough to

use a knife, but she might be able to safely use a good vegetable peeler. Let her wash the vegetables and help measure out the ingredients. Don't rush! Talk about the different ingredients and how they will come together. Enjoy the smells of the food. Let your grandchild have one of the peeled carrots if she wants, or a few of the chocolate chips that fall out of the bag while you are mixing up the batter for dessert.

8 Set the table. Go ahead and get creative: a redchecked tablecloth for an Italian meal, for example, or maybe this occasion will call for your good china. Perhaps your grandchild will enjoy making hand-designed place cards for each guest.

9 Finish cooking, welcome your guests, and enjoy. Don't forget to take some pictures along the way!

Create Your Family Tree

*C*onstructing a family tree with your grandchildren is a wonderful way to help them understand who is related to whom, why it is that they share grandparents with their cousins, that their uncle is their father's brother, and where everyone comes from. It's the perfect activity for taking an abstract notion (genealogy) and giving it tangible form (divergent branches of a tree or linked boxes on a genogram chart). Go as far back as you can, even if it isn't too far; the process itself will still give your grandchildren a good sense of the current family, and your firsthand stories and reminiscences of at least two older generations of family members will help bring the names to life.

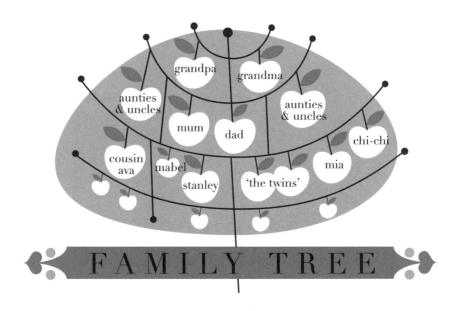

1 On a piece of paper, sketch out the family connections you remember, beginning with your grandchildren and going back to each prior generation, one at a time.

2 You may need to leave some blanks if you cannot remember specific names of family members. Encourage your grandchildren to phone or e-mail their aunts, cousins, and other grandparents to see if they can provide the missing information. Surely someone will remember that great-aunt who lived alone in Vermont all those years.

3 Open up your family photo albums and try to find a picture of each family member on the list. If no photo is available for particular relatives, have your grandchildren draw a representation of them once you map out the actual chart or tree (see step 5).

4 Lay out the poster board and help the children map out the tree design. It's fine to use pencils at first; later the kids can go over the pencil tracings with colorful markers. You may even want to use Post-It squares when you first lay out the design so that the children can see how much space to allot for the entire tree. A typical family tree connects members with links in the form of branches. So, for example, you'll allot one square to your father's name and photo, one square to your mother's, and then draw branches leading from each of those squares to a square just below it with your name and photo in it. If you have siblings, your squares would all be on the same line and would all connect back to your parents, with individual branches leading to squares with the names of your own children and your children's children.

5 Let the kids draw in pictures for any family member for whom you do not have a photograph, and designate to the child with the best penmanship the task of lettering names beneath the appropriate photo or illustration.

6 When the entire tree is finished, you can take the board to a copy shop to create individual paper versions for each child. The trees can be rolled up in scroll form and unfurled so the children can proudly share their project with parents and friends.

Top 10 Books to Read to Your Grandchildren

*E*very family has favorite books they've read so many times the kids can recite them by heart. What follows is a list of one family's top ten, arranged in order from titles for young readers to those for older readers. As your grandchildren mature, they will learn what themes hold their interest best, so you'll ultimately take their cues. But is there really anyone out there who is too old to hear about Dr. Seuss's Once-ler and the Lorax?

1. *More More More Said the Baby* by Vera B. Williams. This board book contains three short stories about babies trying to get away from their caregivers; each time they're scooped up and hugged as the child asks for more.

2. *Silly Sally* by Audrey Wood. In this board book, Sally tries to get to town walking backward and upsidedown and meets with many adventures along the way.

3. *Click, Clack, Moo—Cows That Type* by Doreen Cronin. A picture book about what happens when Farmer Brown's cows get too smart and get hold of a typewriter.

4. *Toot & Puddle* by Holly Hobbie. The charming story about two best friends who happen to be adorable pigs. One wants to travel the world and the other wants to stay home, but more than anything they want to be together.

5. *Miss Spider's Tea Party* by David Kirk. Illustrated with beautiful full-color drawings, this book tells the story of a spider who tries to convince other bugs that her reputation does not properly represent her. All she wants is to have friends. In the end she gets some.

6. *In the Night Kitchen* by Maurice Sendak. A Sendak classic on par with his *Where the Wild Things Are*. Here's the story of Mickey, who wanders into a bakery in the middle of the night. The prose is so much fun to read, you might find yourself reciting it even after the book is back on the shelf.

7. *Skippy Jon Jones* by Judy Schachner. The memorable story of a Siamese cat named Skippy Jon Jones who really wants to be a Chihuahua. He is always making his loving mother angry. When he's sent to his room, he enters his closet—and his adventures begin. Make sure to read it with your very best Spanish accent.

8. *The Lorax* by Dr. Seuss. The classic tale of the Once-ler, who comes to town to cut down the Truffula Trees. He eventually cuts down all the trees and makes it impossible for the native creatures to remain. But there is hope at the end of this timely rhyming book.

9. *Sylvester and the Magic Pebble* by William Steig. A beautiful "be careful what you wish for" book with a very happy ending.

10. *The Trumpet of the Swan* by E. B. White. A great read-aloud chapter book, this is the story of a trumpeter swan who lacks a voice but has an amazing character; ultimately the swan finds happiness and a different sort of voice.

Make Your Own Book

If reading is one of the activities you and your grandchildren enjoy most, consider writing a children's book together: Brainstorm the plot and the characters. If your grandchildren are very young, have them draw the pictures; you can write or type the words. Title the book together and create an "about the authors page." You can keep the binding simple by stapling the pages together or use a hole punch and tie the pages together with yarn. For a more high-tech effect, lay out the book on your computer and scan in the children's illustrations. Some DIY book kits allow you to send out the pages for binding, and some book printers also will print a book for a fee. Your "limited edition" could make a great gift!

Open Up a Bank Account for Your Grandchild

*O*pening a small savings account for and with your grand-children can teach them so much about the value of money, how important it is to save, and how, even by making small deposits every now and then, their savings can add up. Most banks offer plans just for kids that are geared toward making banking more fun; they may include lollipops and toys as well as a low or no minimum deposit.

* Call ahead to make sure the bank offers a program for young bankers. If your bank doesn't, another bank in town might. Look for a bank that is friendly and bright. Some have machines where you can dump your coins and count your money. Others give prizes and have a never-ending candy supply.
* Find out what you have to bring with you to start the account. Some banks require the children's birth certificates and social security cards.
* Find out how the children can deposit money themselves. Some banks even encourage the children to bring loose change to the arcade machine, and then simply transfer that amount to their accounts. They might be able to deposit as little as fifty cents at a time.
* Share the bank statements with your grandchildren. Usually, the statements will be sent to you, but you can make them a copy and send it to them or tell them how much their accounts are growing the next time you talk on the phone. Either way, it will be an ongoing project for you to share, and a lifelong lesson on the importance of saving money.

The Top 10 Questions Every Grandchild Asks

*C*hildren ask a lot of questions, and they look to you to know all the answers. You are, after all, a grandparent, and you *should* know everything by now, right? If you're lucky, they'll ask you the one question you've dedicated your life to answering. (Who makes the best chocolate bar? What's the best time of day to take a nap? Is Michael Jordan the best basketball player who ever lived?) But when you have no idea, go ahead and admit it. Make it a quest for information, then work together to find the answer with some library or online research tools. Meanwhile, review the cheat sheet below so you can be prepared with answers to the top ten most burning questions children want to know.

1. Can owls really turn their heads all the way around? No. But it looks like they do because they can turn their heads more than halfway or even three-quarters of the way around before facing forward again.

2. What is hail and how big can it get? Hail is a form of precipitation, like rain, snow, and freezing rain, but it falls in the shape of balls made mostly of ice. Hail particles come from thunderclouds, and they form when ice crystals are blown back up (sometimes repeatedly) toward the top of the cloud before falling to earth. As they are blown back, the particles collect additional layers of frozen water and become bigger. When they become too heavy for the wind to blow them upward any longer, they fall to earth. The size of hail ranges from a pea to a softball to a small grapefruit.

3. **What is at the center of the earth?** Most people imagine a roiling liquid center at the core of the earth but, although there is hot iron liquid just outside the earth's true center, the central core is thought to be made up mostly of dense, solid iron. The core is extremely hot—perhaps even hotter than the surface of the sun.

4. **Do worms have blood?** Yes. Earthworms are much more complicated and more highly evolved than most people think. Many varieties have red blood with hemoglobin that carries the oxygen throughout their bodies, just as human blood does. A few species have green pigment in their blood, and others have no pigment at all. Other surprising facts: Earthworms also have small brains, eyes, and taste buds.

5. **Where is the world's tallest tree?** The tallest is a redwood tree that stands almost 400 feet tall in the Redwood National Forest in California. It isn't unusual for redwoods to reach as much as 300 feet high.

6. **What is the world's fastest car?** The Ultimate Aero, made by Shelby SuperCars, can go about 257 miles per hour and costs more than $650,000. In 2007 it became the *Guinness Book of World Records'* fastest car.

7. **Why is the sky blue?** Out of all the colors of the rainbow—red, orange, yellow, green, blue, indigo, and violet—blue light waves are toward the short-wavelength end of the visible spectrum. This means the waves are scattered at a greater rate throughout the atmosphere in comparison with the other colors (which have longer wavelengths and are absorbed instead of scattered).

8. **Why do horses sleep standing up?** Because they must be ready to run at all times. This trait is the horse's main defense mechanism in case a predator approaches. It's left over from the time when most horses lived in the wild and could be attacked at any moment by a bear or coyote.

9. **Why do people yawn?** To bring extra oxygen into their bodies. When a person gets tired, the body, including the heart, slows down a bit, so it attempts to bring in more air, and the oxygen within it. Yawning is taking an extra-big gulp of air.

10. **Is there really magic in the world?** That probably depends on whom you ask. Can we transport ourselves the way Harry Potter can? Maybe we will someday. Can we wave a wand, say a spell, and change the world? Not usually. But you can't look at your grandchildren without believing there's got to be a whole lot of magic out there somewhere.

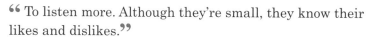

Grandparent Wisdom

WHAT'S THE ONE THING YOU WISH YOU HAD DONE DIFFERENTLY WITH YOUR GRANDCHILDREN?

66 To listen more. Although they're small, they know their likes and dislikes. 99

—Judy, grandmother of 4

66 Don't talk on cell phones when with the grandchildren; they relish your undivided attention. 99

—"Grandma," grandmother of 10

[Not letting them hear] adults talking about adult things. 99

—Nancy, grandmother of 5

66 I had grandparents who were very special—always generous—and I learned from my own parents, who were special grandparents to my children, so I probably would not change very much. I would have liked to have discussed [their parents' divorce] with my grandchildren, but felt I was better off not doing it. I think I have a far better relationship because I did not interfere. When grandchildren want to share their feelings, they will. 99

—Fran, grandmother of 2

66 I wish I had spent more time [with them]. I missed some of their games [but] rarely missed recitals, concerts, plays, and musicals. I wish I could have gone to *all* their activities. 99

—Nancy, grandmother of 4

Metric Conversion Charts

All equivalent measurements and weights have been rounded up or down slightly.

VOLUME

U.S.	Metric
1/4 tsp	1.2 ml
1/2 tsp	2.5 ml
1 tsp	5.0 ml
1 tbsp (3 tsp)	15 ml
1 fl oz (2 tbsp)	30 ml
1/4 cup (4 tbsp)	60 ml
1/3 cup (5 tbsp)	75 ml
1/2 cup (8 tbsp)	125 ml
1 pint (2 cups)	500 ml
1 quart (2 pints)	1 liter

OVEN TEMPERATURE

F	C	Gas Mark
250–275	130–140	1/2–1
300	150	2
325	170	3
350	180	4
375	190	5
400	200	6
425	220	7
450	230	8
475	250	9

WEIGHT

U.S.	Metric
1 oz	30 g
6 oz	175 g
8 oz (1/2 lb)	225 g
12 oz	350 g
16 oz (1 lb)	450 g

LENGTH

Inches	Centimeters
½	1.25
1	2.5
1	2.5
2	5
3	7.5
4	10
5	12.5
6	15
7	17.5
8	20
9	22.5
10	25
12 (1 FT)	30

irreference \ir-'ef-(ə-)rən(t)s\ *n* (2009)

    1 : irreverent reference

    2 : real information that also entertains or amuses

How-Tos. Quizzes. Instructions.
Recipes. Crafts. Jokes.
Trivia. Games. Tricks.
Quotes. Advice. Tips.

Learn something. Or not.

VISIT IRREFERENCE.COM
The New Quirk Books Web Site